HOPE IN THE DARK

ALSO BY REBECCA SOLNIT

Secret Exhibition: Six California Artists of the Cold War Era

A Book of Migrations: Some Passages in Ireland

Savage Dreams: A Journey into the Landscape Wars of the American West

Wanderlust: A History of Walking

Hollow City: The Siege of San Francisco and the Crisis of Urban America

River of Shadows: Eadweard Muybridge and the Technological Wild West

As Eve Said to the Serpent: On Landscape, Gender, and Art

HOPE IN THE DARK

REBECCA SOLNIT

HOPE IN THE DARK

Untold Histories, Wild Possibilities

NATION BOOKS
NEW YORK

HOPE IN THE DARK: UNTOLD HISTORIES, WILD POSSIBILITIES

Published by
Nation Books
An Imprint of Avalon Publishing Group
245 West 17th Street, 11th Floor
New York, NY 10011

Nation Books is a copublishing venture of the Nation
Institute and Avalon Publishing Group Incorporated.

Library of Congress Cataloging-in-Publication Data is available.

ISBN: 1-56025-828-4
ISBN 13: 978-1-56025-828-5

9 8 7 6 5 4 3 2 1

Book design by Simon M. Sullivan

Printed in the United States of America
Distributed by Publishers Group West

Portions of chapters 6 and 9 were published in different form in
Orion Magazine in 2003, while much of chapter 8 originally
appeared in the *San Francisco Chronicle*, September, 2002.

TABLE OF CONTENTS

*"Nothing that has ever happened
should be regarded as lost for history."*

—Walter Benjamin

*"If you don't like the news,
go out and make some of your own."*

—Newsman Wes Nisker's closing salutation
on radio station KTIM in the 1970s

Looking into Darkness

On January 18, 1915, six months into the First World War, as all Europe was convulsed by killing and dying, Virginia Woolf wrote in her journal, "The future is dark, which is on the whole, the best thing the future can be, I think." Dark, she seems to be saying, as in inscrutable, not as in terrible. We often mistake the one for the other. Or we transform the future's unknowability into something certain, the fulfillment of all our dread, the place beyond which there is no way forward. But again and again, far stranger things happen than the end of the world.

Who, two decades ago, could have imagined a world in which the Soviet Union had vanished and the Internet had arrived? Who then dreamed that the political prisoner Nelson Mandela would become president of a transformed South Africa? Who foresaw the resurgence of the indigenous world of which the Zapatista uprising in southern Mexico is only the most visible face? Who, four decades ago, could have conceived of the changed status of all who are nonwhite, nonmale, or nonstraight, the wide-open conversations about power, nature, economies, and ecologies?

There are times when it seems as though not only the future but the present is dark: few recognize what a radically transformed world we live in, one that has been transformed not only by such nightmares as global warming and global capital, but by dreams of freedom and of justice—and transformed by things we could not have dreamed of. We adjust to changes without measuring them, we forget how much the culture has changed. The US Supreme Court ruled in favor of gay rights on a grand scale last summer, a ruling inconceivable a few decades ago. What accretion of incremental, imperceptible changes made that possible, and how did they come about? And so we need to hope for the realization of our own dreams, but also to recognize a world that will remain wilder than our imaginations.

Twenty-one years ago this June, a million people gathered in New York City's Central Park to demand a nuclear freeze. They didn't get it. The freeze movement was full of people who believed they'd realize their goal in a few years and then go home. They were motivated by a story line in which the world would be made safe—safe for, among other things, going home from activism. Many went home disappointed or burned out, though some are still doing great work. But in less than a decade, major nuclear arms reductions were negotiated, helped along by European antinuclear movements and the impetus they gave the Soviet Union's last prime minister, Mikhail Gorbachev. Since then, the issue has fallen off the map and we have lost much of what was gained. The United States never ratified the Comprehensive Test Ban Treaty, which could have put an end to nuclear weapons development and proliferation. Instead, the arms race continues as new nations go nuclear, and the current Bush administration is planning to resume the full-fledged nuclear testing halted in 1991, to resume development of a new generation of nuclear weapons, to expand the arsenal, and perhaps even to use it in once-proscribed ways. The activism of the freeze era cut itself short, with a fixed vision and an unrealistic timeline, not anticipating that the Cold War would come to an end at the close of the decade. They didn't push hard enough or stay long enough to collect the famous peace dividend, and so there was none.

It's always too soon to go home. And it's always too soon to calculate effect. I once read an anecdote by someone involved in Women's Strike for Peace (WSP), the first great antinuclear movement in the United States, the one that did contribute to a major victory: the end, in 1963, of aboveground of nuclear testing and so, of the radioactive fallout that was showing up in mother's milk and baby teeth (and to the fall of the House UnAmerican Activities Committee, the Homeland Security Department of its day. Positioning themselves as housewives and using humor as their weapon, they made HUAC's anticommunist interrogations look ridiculous.) The woman from WSP told of how foolish and futile she had felt standing in the rain one morning protesting at the Kennedy White House. Years later she heard Dr. Benjamin Spock—who had become one of the most high-profile activists on the issue—say that the turning point for him was spotting a small group of women standing in the rain, protesting at the White House. If they were so passionately committed, he thought, he should give the issue more consideration himself.

Causes and effects assume history marches forward, but history is not an army. It is a crab scuttling sideways, a drip of soft water wearing away stone, an earthquake breaking centuries of tension. Sometimes one person inspires a movement, or her words do decades later; sometimes a few passionate people change the world; sometimes they start a mass movement and millions do; sometimes those millions are stirred by the same outrage or the same ideal and change comes upon us like a change of weather. All that these transformations have in common is that they begin in the imagination, in hope. To hope is to gamble. It's to bet on the future, on your desires, on the possibility that an open heart and uncertainty are better than gloom and safety. To hope is dangerous, and yet it is the opposite of fear, for to live is to risk.

I say all this to you because hope is not like a lottery ticket you can sit on the sofa and clutch, feeling lucky. I say this because hope is an ax you break down doors with in an emergency; because hope should shove you out the door, because it will take everything you have to steer the future away from endless war, from the annihilation of the earth's treasures and the grinding down of the poor and marginal. Hope just means another world might be possible, not promised, not guaranteed. Hope calls for action; action is impossible without hope. At the beginning of his massive 1930s treatise on hope, the German philosopher Ernst Bloch wrote, "The work of this emotion requires people who throw themselves actively into what is becoming, to which they themselves belong." To hope is to give yourself to the future, and that commitment to the future makes the present inhabitable.

Anything could happen, and whether we act or not has everything to do with it. Though there is no lottery ticket for the lazy and the detached, for the engaged there is a tremendous gamble for the highest stakes right now. I say this to you not because I haven't noticed that this country has strayed close to destroying itself and everything it once stood for in pursuit of empire in the world and the eradication of democracy at home, that our civilization is close to destroying the very nature on which we depend—the oceans, the atmosphere, the uncounted species of plant and insect and bird. I say it because I *have* noticed: wars will break out, the planet will heat up, species will die out, but how many, how hot, and what survives depends on whether we act. The future is dark, with a darkness as much of the womb as of the grave.

In this book, I want to propose a new vision of how change happens; I want to count a few of the victories that get overlooked; I want to assess the wildly changed world we inhabit; I want to throw out the crippling assumptions with which many activists proceed. I want to start over, with an imagination adequate to the possibilities and the strangeness and the dangers on this earth in this moment.

2

OTHER WAYS OF TELLING

In a photograph, four men lift a two-year-old girl from the rubble of the May 2003 Algerian earthquake as if they were midwives delivering her into the world. The camera of the photographer, Jerome Delay, peers down so that we see mostly the top of the men's heads and their outstretched arms. The girl, Emilie Kaidi, looks up with a grave and open face, ready to be born again into this world that nearly buried her. A lock of black hair cuts across one wide eye to touch her mouth. The photograph isn't really news; the earthquake that killed more than 1,400 Algerians was only a small item here; what happened to her was neither caused by nor overtly affects our own actions. The photograph was probably on the front page of the *San Francisco Chronicle* because it's such a beautiful composition and because the expression on her face is so miraculous, this trust and seriousness from a girl who survived because she called for her mother for two days. It was her cries that let these volunteers from Spain whose hands look so huge locate her.

And when I look at the photograph now, yellowed from months on my refrigerator, I realize that it struck me because of another image that was everywhere that April of 2003: the photograph of Ali Ismaail Abbas, the twelve-year-old Iraqi boy who lost his father, his pregnant mother, fourteen other family members, and both of his arms to American bombing in Baghdad. He, too, had a beautiful face and seemed strangely composed in the most widely seen photograph, looking back at us—from whom came the bombs to mutilate him and make him an orphan. And in the photographs he was alone, though someone must have pulled him, too, from the rubble.

The photograph of Ali Abbas was news. The photograph of Emilie Kaidi was not. What happened to him happened because of politics, because news is about what went wrong, because he tells us about our own effect in the world as she does not. He became an emblem of what we know, of barbarism and brutality, but what is she an emblem of? Surprise? Trust? Hope? The philosopher Alphonso Lingis says, "Hope is hope against the evidence. Hope arises in a break with the past. There is a kind of cut and the past is let go of. There is a difference between simple expectation and hope. One could say 'because I see this is the way things are going, this is the way things have developed, I expect this to happen'; expectation is based on the pattern you see in the past. . . . I think that hope is a kind of birth—it doesn't come out of what went before, it comes out *in spite of* what went before. Abruptly there's a break and there's an upsurge of hope, something turned toward the future." Cynicism and despair are predicated on a prophesy of more of the same, or of decline and fall. Every generation believes it has arrived at some final state of awareness about justice, about politics, about possibility, and then that state implodes or is swept aside, critiqued from a recently unimaginable standpoint. Ours will be, too. There are problems of expectation and of focus.

Survival demands that you notice the tiger in the tree before you pay attention to the beauty of its branches. The one person who's furious at you compels more attention than the eighty-nine who love you. Problems are our work; we deal with them in order to survive or to improve the world, and so to face them is better than turning away from them, than burying them and denying them. To face problems can be an act of hope, but only if you remember that they're not all there is. Some bomb, some dig.

Some of it is a matter of how we tell our stories, the problem of expectation. On April 7, 2003, a few days after American bombs landed on Ali Abbas and his family, several hundred peace activists came out at dawn to picket the gates of a company shipping armaments to Iraq from the docks in Oakland, California. The longshoreman's union had vowed not to cross our picket line. The police arrived in riot gear and, unprovoked and unthreatened, began firing wooden bullets and beanbags of shot at the

activists. They had been instructed to regard us as tantamount to terrorists: "You can make an easy kind of a link
that, if you have a protest group protesting a war where the
cause that's being fought against is international terrorism, you might have terrorism at that [protest]," said
Mike Van Winkle of the California Justice Department.
"You can almost argue that a protest against that is a ter-
rorist act." Three members of the media, nine longshoremen, and fifty activists were injured. I saw bloody
welts the size of half grapefruits on the backs of some of
the young men—they had been shot as they fled—and a
swelling the size of an egg on the jaw of a delicate yoga
instructor. Told that way, violence won.

But the violence also inspired the union dock workers to
form a closer alliance with antiwar activists and under-
scored the connections between local and global issues.
On May 12, we picketed again, with no violence. This time,
the longshoremen acted in solidarity with the picketers
and, for the first time in memory, the shipping companies
cancelled a work shift rather than face protest. Told that
way, the story continued to unfold, and we grew stronger.

And there's a third way to tell it. The April 7 picket
stalled a lot of semi trucks. Some of the drivers were
annoyed. Some—we talked to them—sincerely believed
that the war was a humanitarian effort. Some of them—
notably a group of South Asian drivers standing around in
the morning sun looking radiant—thought we were great.

After the picket was broken up, one immigrant driver honked in support and pulled over to ask for a peace sign for his rig. I stepped forward to pierce holes in it with my pocket knife so he could bungee-cord it to the truck's chrome grille. We talked briefly, shook hands, and he stepped up into the cab. He was turned back at the gates. They weren't accepting deliveries from antiwar truckers. When I next saw the driver, he was sitting on a curb all alone behind police lines, looking cheerful and fearless. Who knows what has or will come of the spontaneous courage of this man with a job on the line?

Ali Abbas was, thanks to the intervention of an Australian journalist, flown to Kuwait and then to Britain for better medical care and prosthetic arms, and chances are good that he will live abroad. The face of a war lives on after the war, as did that girl-child who ran screaming, her flesh burned from American napalm, in what became one of the definitive images of the Vietnam war. The world is full of atrocities now, and it would be criminal to turn our backs on them. Emilie Kaidi's story is not a way to ignore Ali Abbas's story but to move toward it, as the Spaniards moved toward her voice in the ruins; he is news, she is not; together they might be history.

This book tells stories of victories and possibilities because the defeats and disasters are more than adequately documented; it exists not in opposition to or denial of them, but in symbiosis with them, or perhaps as a small counterweight to their tonnage. In the past half century the state of the world has declined dramatically, measured by material terms and by the brutality of wars and economies. But we have also added a huge number of intangibles—rights, ideas, concepts, words to describe and to realize what was once invisible or unimaginable— and these constitute both a breathing space and a toolbox, a toolbox with which those atrocities can be and have been addressed, a box of hope.

I want to illuminate a past that is too seldom recognized, one in which the power of individuals and unarmed people is colossal, in which the scale of change in the world and the collective imagination over the past few decades is staggering, in which the astonishing things that have taken place can brace us to enter that dark future with boldness. To recognize the momentousness of what has happened is to apprehend what might happen. Inside the word *emergency* is emerge; from an emergency new things come forth. The old certainties are crumbling fast, but danger and possibility are sisters.

3

Despair and Discontent,
or THE WALL AND THE DOOR

In *The Principle of Hope*, Bloch declares, "Fraudulent hope is one of the greatest malefactors, even enervators, of the human race, concretely genuine hope its most dedicated benefactor" and speaks of "informed discontent which belongs to hope, because they both arise out of the No to deprivation." The hope that the Publishers Clearing House sweepstakes award will come to you, that the American dream will come true, that electoral politics will reform itself, is hope that paralyzes people's ability to rebel, to reject, to critique, to demand, and to make change. False hope can be a Yes to deprivation, an acquiescence to a lie. Official hope can be the bullying that tells the marginalized to shut up because everything is fine or will be. In its dilute forms, false hope is not so far from despair, for both can be paralyzing. But despair can also be liberating.

Blind hope faces a blank wall waiting for a door in it to open. Doors might be nearby, but blind hope keeps you from locating them; in this geography, despair can be fruitful, can turn you away from the wall, saying No to deprivation. And this despair in one institution or one site can lead to the location of alternatives, to the quest for doors, or to their creation. The great liberation movements hacked doorways into walls, or the walls came tumbling down. In this way, despair and hope are linked.

There are truly desperate circumstances in which hope can—at best—be for bare survival, or that the next atrocity will not take place, or will be confined to certain limits. Hope is a door, or rather a vision of a door, a belief in a way forward that is not open to all people at all times. Yet it sometimes seems that the desperate are more hopeful than the official spokespeople for radical politics—that, say, undocumented immigrants persevere in locating doors while the anointed spokespeople go for the rhetoric of beating one's head against the wall. Despair demands less of us, it's more predictable, and, in a sad way, it's safer.

Sometimes radicals settle for excoriating the wall for being so large, so solid, so blank, so without hinges, knobs, keyholes, rather than seeking a door. Hope, Bloch adds, is in love with success rather than failure, and I'm not sure that's true of a lot of the most audible elements of the Left in this country. The only story many radicals know how to tell is the one that is the underside of the dominant culture's story, more often than not the stuff that never makes it into the news, and all news has a bias in favor of suddenness, violence, and disaster that overlooks groundswells, sea changes, and alternatives. Their premise is: the powers that be are not telling you the whole truth. But the truth *they* tell is *also* incomplete. They conceive of the truth as pure bad news, appoint themselves the deliverers of it, and keep telling it over and over. Eventually, they come to look for the downside in any emerging story, even in apparent victories—and in each other: something about this task seems to give some of them the souls of meter-maids and dogcatchers. (Of course, this also has to do with the nature of adversarial activism, which leads to obsession with the enemy, and, as a few environmentalists have mentioned to me, with the use of alarmist narratives for fund-raising.)

Sometimes these bad-news bringers seem in love with defeat, because if they're constantly prophesying doom, actual doom is, as we say in California, pretty validating. But part of it is a personal style: I think that this grimness is more a psychology than an ideology. There's a kind of activism that's more about bolstering identity than achieving results, one that sometimes seems to make the Left the true heirs of the Puritans. Puritanical in that the point becomes the demonstration of one's own virtue rather than the realization of results. And puritanical because the somber pleasure of condemning things is the most enduring part of that legacy, along with the sense of personal superiority that comes from pleasure denied. . Despair, bad news, grimness bolster an identity the teller can affect, one that is masculine, stern, disillusioned, tough enough to face facts. Some of them, anyway. (Some of the facts remain in the dark.) There are a lot of situations in which the outcome is uncertain, but for some reason tales of decline and fall have an authority that hopeful ones don't. Buddhists sometimes decry hope as an attachment to a specific outcome, to a story line, to satisfaction. But what remains, I think, is an entirely different sort of hope or faith: that you possess the power to change the world to some degree, that the current state of affairs is not inevitable, that all trajectories are not downhill.

Walls can justify being stalled; doors demand passage. Hopefulness is risky, since it is after all a form of trust, trust in the unknown and the possible—even, as Lingis points out, in discontinuity. To be hopeful is to take on a different persona, one that might be considered feminine or childish or sweet. Sometimes despair or grimness calcifies out of honest idealism, disappointed again and again, out of pain at the atrocities unfolding. Other times that tale of gloom seems to come from the belief in a univocal narrative, in the idea that everything is heading in one direction, and since it's clearly not all good, it must be all bad. "Democracy is in trouble," is the phrase with which an eminent activist opens a talk, which is true, but it's also true that it's flourishing in bold new ways in South America and in grassroots movements around the world. It's important to denounce the wall, to describe its obdurate impenetrability.

Before a disease can be treated, it must be diagnosed. But then the question is, what prescription, what cure, what chance of recovery, what alternative?

Political awareness without activism means looking at the devastation, your face turned toward the center of things. Activism can generate hope because in itself it constitutes an alternative and turns away from the corruption at the center to face the wild possibilities and the heroes at the edges or at your side. These ideas of hope are deeply disturbing to a certain kind of presumptive progressive, one who is securely established one way or another. It may simply be that this is not their story, or it may be that hope demands things of them despair does not. Sometimes they regard stories of victory or possibility as hardhearted. Another part of the Puritan legacy is the notion that no one should have joy or abundance until everyone does, a belief that's austere at one end in the deprivation it endorses, and fantastical in the other, since it awaits a universal utopia. Joy sneaks in anyway, abundance cascades forth uninvited. The great human rights activist and Irish nationalist Roger Casement investigated horrific torture and genocide in South America's Putumayo rain forest a century ago. While on this somber task, his journal reveals, he found time to admire handsome local men and to chase brilliantly colored local butterflies. Joy doesn't betray but sustains activism.

Throughout this book I use the word *activist*. Though

there are myriad ways of being an activist, and though
the toil of a daycare worker may be more heroic than that
of a rebel in the street, my emphasis is on direct
engagement. Much of my own experience has been
with civil disobedience, marches, blockades, and other
forms of nonviolent direct action (which is the fruit of
less-direct action—meetings, organizing, networking—
in less-public arenas). An equally important act is the
creation of parallel and alternative institutions, of
turning away from rather than confronting authority and
injustice. Refusal to act also matters tremendously, from
the Israeli pilots who will not fly missions to bomb Pales-
tinians to US Major Charmaine Means, who refused
direct orders to shut down the television station in
Mosul, Iraq, last spring, on the grounds that she was not
in the army to suppress free speech.

This book is an argument that culture generates politics
and that every act counts. Still, I use the term activist to
mean a particular kind of engagement—and a specific
politic: one that seeks to democratize the world, to share
power, to protect difference and complexity, human and
otherwise.

Many people have given up on the most direct
activism, because of its abrasiveness, because of its flawed
participants, because their goal was not realized, or perhaps because a certain incendiary spirit and bodily risk-
taking suits youth best. But not all of them have given up.

Michael Taussig tells a story of a photojournalist in Colombia who, after years of covering the wars in Latin America, "sold all his cameras and has completely given up photography, on the grounds that the camera got between him and people. And what he did was create a tiny foundation to help kids in the immediate four blocks around where he lived—kids who are prostitutes and drug addicts. He goes down every night with a bag full of syringes, condoms and vitamins. . . . What does it mean to shrink from that world of the international media to working four blocks from around your house and in this, one might think, hopeless way—these totally destroyed kids of whom there are so many—and, you know, night after night go out and do the thing with the age difference, the colour difference, the class difference. . . . It seems to me it is a way of life, or generates a way of life, which is a completely different calculus of hope. . . ."

4
What We Won

What initially prompted me to write this book was the despair that followed a season of extraordinary peace activism in the spring of 2003. The despairing could recognize only one victory, the one we didn't grasp, the prevention of the war in Iraq. The Bush administration suggested that the taking of Baghdad constituted victory, but they seem to have conquered neither people nor politics, only infrastructure, for the real war began then, the guerrilla resistance that appears to be growing, and the international fallout that will long be felt. By the fall we had been vindicated in our refusal to believe that Saddam Hussein's regime posed a serious threat to the United States, the United Kingdom, or the world, or harbored serious arsenals of weapons of mass destruction. But being right is small comfort when people are dying and living horribly, as are both the Iraqis in their ravaged land and the poor kids who constitute our occupying army.

At the same time, the peace movement accomplished some significant things that need to be recognized. We will likely never know, but it seems that the Bush administration decided against the "Shock and Awe" saturation bombing of Baghdad because we made it clear that the cost in world opinion and civil unrest would be too high. We millions may have saved a few thousand or a few tens of thousands of lives. The global debate about the war delayed it for months, months that perhaps gave many Iraqis time to lay in stores, evacuate, brace for the onslaught.

Activists are often portrayed as an unrepresentative, marginal rabble, but something shifted in the media in the fall of 2002. Since then, antiwar activists have mostly been represented as a diverse, legitimate, and representative body, a victory for our representation and our long-term prospects.

Many people who had never spoken out, never marched in the street, never joined groups, written to politicians, or donated to campaigns, did so; countless people became political as never before. That is, if nothing else, a vast reservoir of passion now stored up to feed the river of change. New networks and communities and websites and listserves and jail-solidarity groups and coalitions arose and are still with us.

In the name of the so-called war on terror, which seems to inculcate terror at home and enact it abroad, we were encouraged to fear our neighbors, each other, strangers (particularly Middle Eastern, Arab, and Muslim people or people who looked that way), to spy on them, to lock ourselves up, to privatize ourselves. By living out our hope and resistance in public together with strangers of all kinds, we overcame this catechism of fear; we trusted each other; we forged a community that bridged the differences among the peace-loving as we demonstrated our commitment to the people of Iraq.

We achieved a global movement without leaders. There were brilliant spokespeople, theorists, and organizers, but when your fate rests on your leader, you are only as strong, as incorruptible, and as creative as he—or, occasionally, she—is. What could be more democratic than millions of people who, via the grapevine, the Internet, and various assemblies from churches to unions to direct-action affinity groups, can organize themselves? Of course, leaderless actions and movements have been organized for the past couple of decades, but never on such a grand scale. The African writer Laurens Van Der Post once said that no great new leaders were emerging because it was time for us to cease to be followers. Perhaps we have.

Most of us succeeded in refusing the dichotomies. We were able to oppose a war on Iraq without endorsing Saddam Hussein. We were able to oppose a war with compassion for the troops who fought it. Most of us did not fall into the traps that our foreign policy so often does and that earlier generations of radicals sometimes did: the ones in which our enemy's enemy is our friend, in which the opponent of an evil must be good, in which a nation and its figurehead, a general and his troops, become indistinguishable. We were not against the United States and for Iraq; we were against the war, and many of us were against all war, all weapons of mass destruction, and all violence, everywhere. We are not just an antiwar movement. We are a peace movement.

Questions the peace and global justice movements have raised are now mainstream, though no mainstream source will say why, or perhaps even knows why. Activists targeted Bechtel, Halliburton, Chevron-Texaco, and Lockheed Martin, among others, as war profiteers with ties to the Bush administration. These actions worked not by shutting the places down in any significant way but by making their operations open to public question. Direct action seldom works directly, but now the media scrutinizes those corporations as never before.

Gary Younge writes in the British *Guardian*, "The anti-war movement got the German chancellor, Gerhard Schröder, re-elected, and has pushed the center of gravity in the Democratic primaries in a more progressive direction. Political leaders need not only geographical but also ideological constituencies. Over the past two years the Left has built a strong enough base to support those who chose to challenge American hegemony. True, none of this has

saved Iraqi lives. But with ratings for Bush and Blair plummeting, it may keep Iranians, North Koreans or whoever
else they are considering bombing out of harm's way."

None of these victories are comparable to the victory
that preventing the war would have been—but if the war
had indeed been prevented, the Bush and Blair administrations would have supplied elaborate explanations that
had nothing to do with public opinion and international
pressure, and many would still believe that we had had no
impact. The government and the media routinely dis-
count the effect of activists, but there's no reason we
should believe them, or let them tally our victories for us.
To be effective, activists have to make strong, simple,
urgent demands, at least some of the time—the kinds of
demands that fit on stickers and placards, the kinds that
can be shouted in the street by a thousand people. And
they have to recognize that their victories may come as
subtle, complex, slow changes instead, and count them
anyway. A love of paradox is not the least of the equip
ment any activist should have.

And there's one more victory worth counting. The
global peace movement was grossly underreported on
February 15, 2003, when somewhere between eleven and
thirty million people marched and demonstrated on every
continent, including the scientists at McMurdo Station in
Antarctica. A million people marching in Barcelona was
nice, but I also heard about the thousands in Chapel Hill,

North Carolina, the hundred and fifty people holding a peace vigil in the small town of Las Vegas, New Mexico, the antiwar passion of people in even smaller villages in Bolivia, in Thailand, in Inuit northern Canada. George W. Bush campaigned as a uniter, not a divider, and he very nearly united the whole world against the administrations of the United States and Britain. Those tens of millions on every continent constituted something unprecedented, one of the ruptures that have ushered in a new era. I want to count down to that day.

5

THE MILLENNIUM ARRIVES:
NOVEMBER 9, 1989

I was born the summer the Berlin Wall went up, into a world shadowed by the cold war between the United States of America and the USSR. Many people then believed that a nuclear war was imminent and that such a war could mean the end of the world. People have always been good at imagining the end of the world, which is much easier to picture than the strange sidelong paths of change in a world without end. In the early sixties, international politics seemed deadlocked, but elsewhere things were stirring. The civil rights movement had already transformed the status quo into a crisis, not only for the officials dealing with demonstrators, but for Americans whose conscience had woken up or whose patience had worn out.

That year Women's Strike for Peace was founded when a hundred thousand women in a hundred communities across the country staged a simultaneous one-day strike, launching an antinuclear peace movement that also prefigured the women's movement, soon to be born. That year, Cesar Chavez was considering leaving his community-organizer job to try to unionize California's farmworkers and the science writer Rachel Carson was finishing *Silent Spring*, her landmark denunciation of pesticides, published in 1962. Just as the civil rights movement achieved not only specific gains but a change in the imagination of race and justice, so Carson's book was instrumental not only in getting DDT banned—which reversed the die-off of many bird species—but also in launching a worldview in which nature was made up not of inert objects but of interactive, interconnected systems, a worldview that would come to be called "ecological." Step by step, ecological ideas have entered the mainstream to transform our imagination of the earth and its processes, of fire, water, air, soil, species, interdependences, biodiversities, watersheds, food chains (these latter words also entered the common vocabulary in recent times).

I was born into a world in which there was little or no recourse—and often not even the words—for racial profiling, hate crimes, domestic violence, sexual harassment, homophobia, and other forms of exclusion and oppression. Some of the Ivy League universities did not admit women, and many of the southern colleges and universities admitted only whites. It was a world where the scope for decisions about religion, sexuality, living arrangements, food, and consumption patterns was far narrower, though there were also many old ways of life disappearing.

Pristine wildernesses, family farms, small businesses, independent media, local customs, and indigenous practices were under seige by the homogenizations, consolidations, and commercializations that would supernova as corporate globalization. The very premises from which to resist these eradications were still mostly embryonic. This is the way the world changes, as Dickens understood when he opened his most political novel with "It was the best of times, it was the worst of times." It usually is.

What gets called "the sixties" left a mixed legacy and a lot of divides. But it opened everything to question, and what seems the most fundamental and most pervasive in all the ensuing changes is the loss of faith in authority: the authority of government, of science, of patriarchy, of progress, of capitalism, of violence, of whiteness. The answers—the alternatives—haven't always been clear or easy, but the questions and the questioning are nevertheless significant. What's most important here is to feel the profundity of the changes, to feel how far we have come from that moment of cold-war summer. We inhabit, in ordinary daylight, a future that was unimaginably dark a few decades ago, when people found the end of the world easier to envision than the impending changes—in everyday roles, thoughts, practices—that not even the wildest science fiction anticipated. Perhaps we should not have adjusted to it so easily. It would be better if we were astonished every day.

•   •   •

I was born the summer the Berlin Wall went up, and I
cried when I saw live footage of it coming down twenty-
eight years later, on November 9, 1989. The massive wall
had seemed eternal, like the Cold War itself, and the East
Germans streaming across and the people celebrating in
the streets were amazed, delighted, moved beyond imagining. East German authorities had given permission for
orderly traffic across the wall, not for its eradication as a
boundary—it was because so many people showed up on
both sides that the guards surrendered control altogether.
It was a year of miracles, if change wrought by determination against overwhelming odds can be a miracle. In
May the students of Tiananmen Square had mounted a
direct challenge to the authority of the Chinese government, and though they were defeated, they were only the
first of a series of revolutions, or revelations. At the end of
1989, Nelson Mandela was released from his South
African prison after almost three decades behind bars.
Eastern Europe liberated itself that fall. In the wake of the
collapse of the Soviet Bloc, the Soviet Union collapsed,
too, or rather was dismantled by the will of the people and
the guidance of the extraordinary prime minister, Mikhail
Gorbachev, and his will to give up power. Some of the
revolutions came about as the result of increasingly bold
democratic organizing, notably that of the Solidarity
movement in Poland, where free elections were held that

June after a decade of careful groundwork. But others were more surprising, more spontaneous. The marches in the streets, the people's insistence on exercising their rights as citizens, the sudden coming to voice of the voiceless, were central acts in a moment when a world order seemed at the edge of collapse. By acting as if they were free, the people of Eastern Europe became free.

Often the road to the future leads through the past. Thus it was that in Hungary and Czechoslovakia marches commemorating political martyrs turned into nonviolent revolutions freeing the living. Often the road to politics lies through culture. It was, for example, the 1976 persecution of the Czech band The Plastic People of the Universe that sparked Charter 77, the defiant manifesto issued on New Year's Day, some of whose signatories were key players in 1989. "It was not a bolt out of the blue, of course," wrote Charter 77 signatory and playwright Václav Havel long before he became president of a post-communist Czechoslovakia, "but that impression is understandable, since the ferment that led to it took place in the 'hidden sphere,' in that semi-darkness where things are difficult to chart or analyse. The chances of predicting the appearance of the Charter were just as slight as the chances are now of predicting where it will lead."

One could trace the equally strange trajectory that created rock and roll out of African and Scots-Irish musical traditions in the American South, then sent rock and roll around the world, so that a sound that had once been endemic to the South was intrinsic to dissent in the European East. Or the ricocheting trajectory by which Thoreau, abolitionists, Tolstoy, women suffragists, Gandhi, Martin Luther King Jr., and various others had, over the course of more than a century, wrought a doctrine of civil disobedience and nonviolence that would become standard liberatory equipment in every part of the world. If atomic bombs are the worst invention of the twentieth century, this practice might be the best, as well as the antithesis of those bombs. Or perhaps the music should be counted, too. (That both the civil rights movement and the music came out of the African-American South to change the world suggests a startling, resistant richness under all that poverty and oppression and suggests, yet again, the strange workings of history.)

The new era in which we're living did not come into being on the uneventful day of January 1, 2000 (or 2001 for those who are picky about calendrical time). It came into being in stages, and it is still being born, but each of my five dates—in 1989, 1994, 1999, 2001, 2003—constitutes a labor pang, an emergence out of emergency. The millennium was long anticipated as a moment of arrival, as the end of time, but it is instead a beginning of sorts, for something that is increasingly recognizable but yet unnamed, yet unrecognized—a new ground for hope.

6

THE MILLENNIUM ARRIVES:
JANUARY 1, 1994

On New Year's Day in 1994, a guerrilla army of indigenous men, women, and children came out from their hiding places in the Lacandon jungle and mountains of Chiapas, Mexico's southern-most state, and took the world by surprise and six towns by storm. In honor of Emiliano Zapata, another indige-nous Mexican rebel at the other end of the twentieth century, they called themselves the Zapatistas and their philosophy Zapatismo. The fall of the Soviet Bloc was framed as the triumph of capitalism; capitalists increased their assertions that the "free market" was tantamount to democracy and freedom; and the 1990s would see the rise of neoliberalism (the cult of unfettered international capitalism and privatization of goods and services behind what gets called globalization and might more accurately be called corporate globalization). The Zapatistas chose to rise on the day that the North American Free Trade Agreement (NAFTA) went into effect, opening US, Mex-ican, and Canadian borders. They recognized what a decade has proved: NAFTA was an economic death sentence for hundreds of thousands of small-scale Mexican farmers and with them, something of rural and traditional life.

In dazzling proclamations and manifestos, the Zapatistas announced the rise of the fourth world and their radical rejection of neoliberalism. They were never much of a military force, but their intellectual and imaginative power has been staggering. As radical historian and activist Elizabeth Martinez notes, "Zapatismo rejects the idea of a vanguard leading the people. Instead it is an affirmation of communal people's power, of grassroots autonomy. . . . The Zapatistas say they are not proposing to take power but rather to contribute to a vast movement that would return power to civil society, using different forms of struggle." They came not just to enact a specific revolution but to bring a revolution, so to speak, in the nature of revolutions. They critiqued the dynamics of power, previous revolutions, capitalism, colonialism, militarism, sexism, racism, and occasionally Marxism, recognizing the interplay of many forces and agendas in any act, any movement. They were nothing so simple as socialists, and they did not posit the old vision of state socialism as a solution to the problems of neoliberalism. They affirmed women's full and equal rights, refusing to be the revolution that sacrifices or postpones one kind of justice for another. They did not attempt to export their revolution but invited others to find their own local version of it, and from their forests and villages they entered into conversation with the world through *encuentros*, or encounters—conferences of a sort—communiqués, emissaries, and correspondence. For the rest of us, the Zapatistas came as a surprise and as a demonstration that overnight, the most marginal, overlooked place can become the center of the world.

They were not just demanding change, but embodying it; and in this, they were and are already victorious. *"Todo para todos, nada para nosotros,"* is one of their maxims— "Everything for everyone, nothing for ourselves," and though, ten years later, they have more survived than won their quarrel with the Mexican government, they have set loose glorious possibilities for activists everywhere. They understood the interplay between physical actions, those carried out with guns, and symbolic actions, those carried out with words, with images, with art, with communications, and they won through the latter means what they never could have won through their small capacity for violence. Some of their guns were only gun-shaped chunks of wood, as though the Zapatistas were actors in a pageant, not soldiers in a war. This brilliantly enacted pageant caught the hearts and imaginations of Mexican civil society and activists around the world.

The Zapatistas came down from the mountains masked in bandannas and balaclavas, and though most of them were small of stature and dark-eyed, their spokesman was a tall, green-eyed intellectual who spoke several languages and smoked a pipe through the black balaclava he has never been seen without. Subcommandante Marcos, who came several years before 1994 to liberate the *campesinos* and was liberated from the conventionally leftist ideology with which he arrived, is the composer of a new kind of political discourse. For Marcos's is one of the great literary voices of our time, alternately allegorical, paradoxical, scathing, comic, and poetic, and his writings found their way around the world via a new medium, the Internet. His words express not his own ideas alone, exactly—after all, he claims to be a subordinate, a *subcommandante*, and remains masked and pseudonymous—but those of a community bringing into being what those words propose. A singular voice that is a trumpet for a community, a writer composing a bridge across the gap between thoughts and acts.

Zapatista scholar and activist Manuel Callahan points out that the Zapatistas did not come to turn back the clock to some lost indigenous dreamtime, but to hasten the arrival of the future: "We Indian peoples have come in order to wind the clock and to thus ensure that the inclusive, tolerant, and plural tomorrow which is, incidentally, the only tomorrow possible will arrive," Marcos has said. "In order to do that, in order for our march to make the clock of humanity march, we Indian peoples have resorted to the art of reading what has not yet been written. Because that is the dream which animates us as indigenous, as Mexicans and, above all, as human beings. With our struggle, we are reading the future which has already been sown yesterday, which is being cultivated today, and which can only be reaped if one fights, if, that is, one dreams."

Elsewhere, in uncharacteristally straightforward terms, he defined what the Zapatistas were not, if not exactly what they are, saying that if the army they initially appeared to be "perpetuates itself as an armed military structure, it is headed for failure. Failure as an alternative set of ideas, an alternative attitude to the world. The worst that could happen to it, apart from that, would be to come to power and install itself as a revolutionary army. For us it would be a failure. What would be a success for the politico-military organizations of the sixties or seventies which emerged with the national liberation movements would be a fiasco for us. We have seen that such victories proved in the end to be failures, or defeats, hidden behind the mask of success. That what always remained unresolved was the role of people, of civil society, in what became ultimately a dispute between two hegemonies."

There is an amazing moment in George Orwell's *Homage to Catalonia*, his account of his participation in the Spanish Civil War and of the internal feuds between the anarchists and communists that undermined their resistance to the Fascists, who won (with the help of Hitler and Mussolini). Orwell was too rigorously honest a man to toe any political line well; he was always noting the flaws in the ideologies—it was as though he was incapable of keeping his mind on a sufficient plane of abstraction, where ideology and rhetoric fly most freely. In his account of the trench warfare between the Fascists and the loyalist anarchists, he wrote about the slogans the two sides shouted back and forth. The anarchists would shout out slogans, in Orwell's words, "full of revolutionary senti-ments which explained to the Fascist soldiers that they were merely the hirelings of international capitalism, that they were fighting against their own class, etc., etc., and urged them to come over to our side. . . . There is very little doubt it had its effect; everyone agreed that the trickle of Fascist deserters was partly caused by it."

Orwell says the man who did the main shouting on his side "was an artist at the job. Sometimes, instead of shouting revolutionary slogans he simply told the Fascists how much better we were fed than they were. His account of the Goverment rations was apt to be a little imaginative. 'Buttered toast!'—you could hear his voice echoing across the lonely valley—'We're just sitting down to hot buttered toast over here! Lovely slices of buttered toast!' I do not doubt that, like the rest of us, he had not seen butter for weeks or months past, but in the icy night the news of buttered toast probably set many a Fascist mouth watering. It even made mine water, though I knew he was lying."

Those shouts about toast in the trenches prefigure the political speech of the current era, of a playful language whose meaning is more than literal and is more generous than ideology, an invitation rather than an order or a condemnation. You might say that the Spaniard yelling about toast wasn't lying but composing, composing a literature of the trenches, transcending propaganda to make art. And I wonder if what he said was this: that the anarchists were more humane than the fascists because they recognized that beneath the abstractions of political rhetoric are desires that are concrete, real, bodily, because they left room for improvisation and playfulness, pleasure and independence. The anarchic rhetoric of hot buttered toast is Marcos's language of evocation, description, parable, and paradox, full of words that describe things—of birds, bread, blood, clouds—and of words of the heart, of love, dignity, and particularly hope. Its humor recognizes ironies, impossibilities, and disproportions. It is the language of the vast, nameless current movement that globalization has drawn together, a movement or movements driven by imaginations as supple as art rather than as stiff as dogma.

On January 1, 1996, the Fourth Declaration of the Lacondon Jungle was issued. It reads in part, "A new lie is being sold to us as history. The lie of the defeat of hope, the lie of the defeat of dignity, the lie of the defeat of humanity. . . . In place of humanity, they offer us the stock market index. In place of dignity, they offer us the globalization of misery. In place of hope, they offer us emptiness. In place of life, they offer us an International of Terror. Against the International of Terror that neoliberalism represents, we must raise an International of Hope. Unity, beyond borders, languages, colors, cultures, sexes, strategies and thoughts, of all those who prefer a living humanity. The International of Hope. Not the bureaucracy of hope, not an image inverse to, and thus similar to, what is annihilating us. Not power with a new sign or new clothes. A flower, yes, that flower of hope."

The Zapatista uprising was many kinds of revolution, was a green stone thrown in water whose ripples are still spreading outward, a flower whose weightless seeds have been taken up by the wind.

7

The Millennium Arrives: November 30, 1999

s the end of the twentieth century approached, many people became preoccupied with the Y2K problem—with the theory that computers that had not been programmed to deal with four-digit year changes would somehow disable themselves at the stroke of midnight on 12/31/99, and the systems upon which we depend would crash. It was exemplary of a certain radical mindset, morbidity made attractive by anticipated vindication. It never came to pass, of course, but it was good for water and battery sales, and another kind of systemic crash came, a month earlier.

I remember walking the streets of Seattle on November 30, 1999, thinking that the millennium was already here, feeling that enormous exhilaration of consciously living in history. For all around, in intersection after intersection of the gridded, gritty old downtown, people had blockaded the World Trade Organization meeting. There were union and agricultural and human rights activists, environmentalists, anarchists, religious groups, students, and grandparents.

The WTO had been founded to control international trade, and more importantly, to suppress or outlaw all other powers to limit and manage this trade. Though those who oppose it are sometimes called "globophobes" or "anti-globalization" activists, the term globalization can apply to many kinds of internationalization and border crossing, and what we oppose is more accurately called corporate globalization and its ideology, neoliberalism, or sometimes capitalism altogether. (Thus, the movement is now sometimes called anticapitalism, though it is more complex, is for more things, and is less like classical Marxism or socialism than that term suggests—I like the term "global justice movement" for this swarm of resistances and inspirations. Another way to boil down the essential principles would focus on the privatizations and consolidations of power corporate globalization represents and sees the resistance to it as, simply, a struggle to redemocratize the world, or the corner of it from which a given struggle is mounted.)

After all, this form of globalization would essentially suspend local, regional, and national rights of self-determination over labor, environmental, and agricultural conditions in the name of the dubious benefits of the free market, benefits that would be enforced by unaccountable transnational authorities acting primarily to protect the rights of capital. At a recent labor forum, Dave Bevard, a laid-off US union metalworker, referred to this new world order as "government of the corporations, by the corporations, for the corporations." Much of what free trade has brought about is what gets called "the race to the bottom," the quest for the cheapest possible wages or agricultural production, with consequent losses on countless fronts. The argument is always that such moves make industry more profitable, but it would be more accurate to say that it concentrates profit away from workers and communities, for whom it is therefore far less profitable. (And the very term *profit* cries out for redefinition, for the stock market defines as "profitable" every kind of destruction, and lacks terms for valuing cultures, diversities, or long-term well-being, let alone happiness, beauty, freedom, or justice.)

The corporate agenda of NAFTA and related globalization treaties is demonstrated most famously by the case of MTBE, a gasoline additive that causes severe damage to human health and the environment. When California banned it, the Canadian corporation Methanex filed a lawsuit demanding nearly a billion dollars in compensation from the US government for profit lost because of the ban. Under NAFTA rules, corporations have an absolute right to profit with which local laws must not interfere. Poisoning the well is no longer a crime, but stopping the free flow of poison meets with punishment. Other examples of this kind of globalization include the attempts by multinational corporations to privatize water supplies and to patent

genes, including the genes of wild and traditionally cultivated plants—to lock up as commodities much of the basic
stuff of life, all in the name of free trade.

Young global justice advocates understand that, as is
often said, globalization is war by other means. War is easy
to abhor, but it takes a serious passion to unravel the tan-
gles of financial manipulations and to understand the
pain of sweatshop workers or displaced farmers. And
maybe this is what heroism looks like nowadays: occasionally high-profile heroism in public but mostly just
painstaking mastery of arcane policy, stubborn persever-
ence year after year for a cause, empathy with those who
remain unseen, and outrage channeled into dedication.
There had been opposition to corporate globalization
before, most notably the Zapatista uprising on the day
that NAFTA went into effect. But Seattle gathered the
growing momentum and made it impossible to ignore.

Economic historian Charles Derber writes, "The
excitement of Seattle was the subliminal sense that a new
opposition, and perhaps a whole new kind of politics, was
being born, both in the United States and the world at
large . . . . Seattle was mainly a group of white folks. Yet,
and this was very important, there were people from
India, Mexico, the Philippines, and Indonesia. They represented influential groups and millions of people who
had protested on their own streets but couldn't come to
Seattle. So if one looks at the larger movement and the

swelling of the ranks of globalization activists around the world, one would have to conclude that this is truly a crossnational movement and very possibly the first truly global movement." French farmer and revolutionary Jose Bové, who was also there, had a similar response: "I had the feeling that a new period of protest was about to begin in America—a new beginning for politics, after the failures and inactivities of the previous generation."

The global justice movement brought to the progressive/radical community what had long been missing: a comprehensive analysis that laid the groundwork for a broad coalition, for the common ground so absent from the movements of the 1970s and 1980s, which seemed to advance a single sector or pit one issue against another. This is, of course, in part because the globalizing corporations manage to be antienvironmental, antidemocratic, and a whole lot of other atrocities all at once. But the antiglobalization movement, in its breadth, in its flexibility, and its creativity seems, like the Zapatistas, a great step toward reinventing revolution. The year the Zapatistas stepped onto the world stage, the radical geographer Iain Boal had prophesied, "The longing for a better world will need to arise at the imagined meeting place of many movements of resistance, as many as there are sites of closure and exclusion. The resistance will be as transnational as capitalism." That resistance had appeared before Seattle, but it was in that upper left corner of the

United States that it made its transnational presence impossible to ignore.

Fifty thousand people joined the union-led march, and ten thousand activists blockaded the downtown streets, disrupting and ultimately cancelling the meeting of the WTO that day. The shutdown encouraged impoverished-nation delegates and the representatives of non-governmental organizations to stand their ground inside the WTO talks. This time victory—the shutdown—was tangible and immediate. But the action also served to galvanize the world with an unanticipated revolt on a grand scale, and it made corporate globalization a subject of debate as it had not been before.

In Seattle on those two days, there were police riots, police brutality, injuries, hospitalizations, and arrests in violation of First Amendment rights. The famous solidarity— "teamsters and turtles" for the union members and the sea-turtle-costumed environmentalists—did not preclude alienations and infightings. Seattle is sometimes misremembered as an Eden. It was just a miracle, a messy one that won't happen the same way again. Since the Seattle surprise, it's become standard practice to erect a miniature police state around any globalization summit, and these rights-free zones seem to prefigure what corporate globalization promises.

But at the end of November 1999, the media, which had dozed through the massive antinuclear, antiwar, and environmental actions of the eighties and nineties, woke up with a start to proclaim this shutdown the biggest thing since the sixties. In a way it was, in part because they made it so, in part because it was the next phase—built upon the failures and successes of that era. Eddie Yuen points out in the introduction to his anthology *The Battle of Seattle*, "One of the most influential strands of the new movement is the tradition of mass civil disobedience commonly known as Non-Violent Direct Action (NVDA). This tendency . . . was manifested in Seattle in a form that crystallized in the peace and antinuclear movements of the '70s and '80s. This iteration of NVDA is characterized by two principles that have long been assumed to be inseparable, but which may in fact be linked by historical contingency. The first of these is the adoption of a strict nonviolence code that was a response to a macho fascination with revolutionary violence in the '60s. The second is the commitment to direct democracy, as specifically the organizational forms of the affinity group, decentralized spokes-council meetings and consensus process. This commitment was a response to the preponderance of charismatic (and almost always male) leadership cults as well as the increasingly authoritarian organizational forms that became popular during the late New Left."

That is to say, the movement was plural; it came from many directions—among them a constructive critique of the failures of the 1960s and an ethics of power. So you could say that Seattle arose not only from addressing the problem that is "them"—the corporations and governments —but from the problems that have often been "us," the activists, the Left, the revolution. Its success came out of addressing both of these fronts, a response many years in the making. And out of the moment.

Perhaps you've forgotten that in 1999 the arrogance of the boom years was still upon us; corporate CEOs were treated like rock stars; business journalists babbled that the market could go up forever without going down. Then the technology bubble burst; the Enron and Worldcom scandals broke, demonstrating that the corporations were morally bankrupt, too; Argentina went bust thanks to its adherence to neoliberal fiscal policies, ran though several governments, defaulted on its loans, and remains today a place of great economic crisis and greater anarchic social innovation. A decade after communism collapsed, capitalism was a wreck.

"We are winning," said the graffiti in Seattle.

8

THE MILLENNIUM ARRIVES:
SEPTEMBER 11, 2001

The airplanes become bombs were from any perspective a terrible thing. But there was a moment when something beautiful might have come out of it, not only the heroism of those on site, but of those across the country. A President Gore, a President Nader would not have been adequate to the moment. To imagine a leader who could have risen to the occasion, you'd have to reach further, to a President LaDuke or to a parallel universe with a President Martin Luther King. Of course there were belligerent and racist and jingoistic reactions, but there was a long moment when almost everyone seemed to pause, an opening when the nation might have taken another path. And some took that path anyway. I wrote at the time, "In the hours and days that followed everyone agreed that the world was changed, though no one knew exactly how. It was not just the possibility of a war, but the sense of the relation between self and world that changed, at least for Americans.

"To live entirely for oneself in private is a huge luxury,

a luxury countless aspects of this society encourage, but like a diet of pure fois gras it clogs and narrows the arteries of the heart. This is what we're encouraged to crave in this country, but most of us crave more deeply something with more grit, more substance. Since my home county was faced with a disastrous drought when I was fifteen, I have been fascinated by the way people rise to the occasion of a disaster. In that drought, the wealthy citizens of that county enjoyed self-denial for the public good more than they enjoyed private abundance the rest of the time. The 1989 Loma Prieta quake shook San Francisco into the here and now: I remember how my anger at someone suddenly ceased to matter, and so did my plans. The day after the quake, I walked around town to see people I cared about and the world was local and immediate. Not just because the Bay Bridge was damaged and there were practical reasons to stay home, but because the long-term perspective from which so much dissatisfaction and desire comes was shaken too: life, meaning, value were close to home, in the present. We who had been through the quake were present and connected. Connected to death, to fear, to the unknown, but in being so connected one could feel empathy, passion, and heroism as well. We could feel strongly, and that is itself something hard to find in the anesthetizing distractions of this society.

"That first impulse everywhere on September 11 was to give blood, a kind of secular communion in which people offered up the life of their bodies for strangers. The media dropped its advertisements, leers, and gossip and told us about tragedy and heroism. Giving blood and volunteering were the first expression of a sense of connection; the flag became an ambiguous symbol of that connection, since it meant everything from empathy to belligerence. In Brooklyn that week, a friend reported, 'Nobody went to work and everybody talked to strangers.' What makes people heroic and what makes them feel members of a community? I hoped that one thing to come out of the end of American invulnerability would be a stronger sense of what disasters abroad—massacres, occupations, wars, famines, dictatorships—mean and feel like, a sense of citizenship in the world.

"There were spectacular heroes in this disaster, the firefighters, police, medical and sanitation workers who did what could be done at the site afterward and those who died trying in those first hours. But I mean *heroism* as a comparatively selfless state of being and as a willingness to do. Wartime and disaster elicit this heroism most strongly, though there are always volunteers who don't wait until disaster comes home, the volunteers and activists who engage with issues that don't affect them directly, with land mines, discrimination, genocide, the people who want to extend their own privilege and security to those who lack them. In its mildest form that heroism is simply citizenship, a sense of connection and commitment to the community, and for a few months after 9/11 we had a strange surge of citizenship in this country.

"Shortly after the bombing, the president swore to 'eliminate evil' from the world, and with this he seemed to promise that the goodness that filled us would not be necessary in the future, a future in which we could return to preoccupation with our private lives. Though oil politics had much to do with what had happened, we were not asked to give up driving, or vehicles that gulp huge amounts of fuel; we were asked to go shopping, and to spy on our neighbors."

It seemed as though the Bush administration recognized this extraordinary possibility of the moment and did everything it could to suppress it, for nothing is more dangerous to them than that sense of citizenship, fearlessness, and communion with the world (that is distinct from blind patriotism driven by fear). They used 9/11 as an excuse to launch attacks inside and outside the United States, but it was not an inevitable or even a legitimate response—in fact, 9/11 was largely an excuse to carry out existing agendas of imperial expansion and domestic repression. Bush the First had neglected the chances the end of the Cold War gave us, and his son made the worst of the invitations this new emergency offered. I wish 9/11 had not happened, but I wish that the reaction that hovered on the brink of being born had.

9

THE MILLENNIUM ARRIVES:
FEBRUARY 15, 2003

O r perhaps that moment did come, eighteen months later, when we marched against the Iraq war on all the continents of the earth, a *we* that is the antithesis of Bush's post-9/11 proclamation that "you're either with us or against us." Organized via the Internet without leaders or a single ideology, this unprecedented global wave of protest demonstrated the decentralizing political power of that medium, and like Seattle in 1999 it countered the Internet's disembodied placelessness with bodies come together in thousands of cities and in places that weren't urban at all. A march is when bodies speak by walking, when private citizens become that mystery "the public," when traversing the boulevards of cities becomes a way to travel toward political goals. It answered that moment of murder and division on 9/11 with a moment of communion around the world, a moment of trust between the strangers who marched together, a moment when history would be made not by weapons and secrets but by walkers under the open sky.

What was most remarkable about the huge peace marches in San Francisco was the sense of ebullience and exhilaration, as though people had finally found something they'd long craved—a chance to speak out, to participate, to see that others shared their beliefs, to be saying these things someplace where it might matter rather than murmuring about them in private. It was moving and disconcerting to realize that these experiences —of democracy and of citizenship—were so unusual and so desired. Most of the tens of thousands of signs were homemade, and most were beautiful or funny or scathing. Each of the signs was simple in itself, but by the thousands they constituted a sophisticated marshaling of all the arguments against a war in Iraq. I saw a group of Palestinian women on the north side of the street, demure in wool challis head scarves, and directly across from them but screened off by the hordes who streamed by were two young women, one white, one Asian, holding signs depicting your basic scribbled female pubic triangle, inscribed "This Bush for Peace." There was, it seemed, room for everyone.

Periodically a huge roar would go up from the crowd, a roar with no cause I could ever locate, as though the mass of people had become one huge beast reveling in a power that was not violence but strength. With between eleven and thirty million participants around the globe, it was the biggest and most widespread collective protest the world has ever seen, and if you count the small demonstration at McMurdo Station in Antarctica, the first to reach all seven continents. As Archbishop Desmond Tutu pointed out from Manhattan, it was unprecedented to have such broad action against a war that had yet to begin. And there, in Manhattan, where the World Trade Towers had collapsed seventeen months before, more than four hundred thousand people gathered illegally—no march permit was ever issued, and they gathered anyway—to refuse to endorse the revenge being exacted for that crime (for those who credulously believed that Iraq was somehow linked to Al Qaeda). The *New York Times* called the peace movement "the world's other superpower." 9/11 had been a moment of communion born out of atrocity, but this one was born out of insurgency and outraged idealism. It bore witness to a usually unspoken desire for something other than ordinary private life, for something more risky, more involved, more idealistic. Perhaps many—or most—are not really ready to live up to that desire, but it is there, an aquifer of pure passion.

At an event that March, Robert Muller, a peace activist and former assistant secretary general of the United Nations, astounded an audience anticipating war with his optimism. He exclaimed, "I'm so honored to be alive at such a miraculous time in history. I'm so moved by what's going on in our world today. Never before in the history of the world has there been a global, visible, public, viable, open dialogue and conversation about the very legitimacy of war." Journalist Lynne Twist reports that he added, "'All of this is taking place in the context of the United Nations Security Council, the body that was established in 1949 for exactly this purpose.' He pointed out that it has taken us more than fifty years to realize that function, the real function of the U.N. . . . Dr. Muller was almost in tears in recognition of the fulfillment of this dream."

The dream did not last, though the moment is worth cherishing. Instead came the nightmare of burned and maimed children; bombed civilians; soldiers incinerated by depleted-uranium rounds; history itself wiped out, when the United States permitted the looting of Baghdad's National Museum and the burning of its National Library; US soldiers picked off a few at a time during the months of occupation and insurrection. The millions marching on February 15 represented something that is not yet fully realized, an extraordinary potential waiting, waiting for some catalyst to bring it into full flower. A new imagination of politics and change is already here, and I want to try to pare away what obscures it.

10

CHANGING THE IMAGINATION OF CHANGE

A lot of activists seem to have a mechanistic view of change, or perhaps they expect what quack diet pills offer, "Quick and easy results guaranteed." They expect finality, definitiveness, straightforward cause-and-effect relationships, instant returns, and as a result they specialize in disappointment, which sinks in as bitterness, cynicism, defeatism, knowingness. They operate on the premise that for every action there is an equal and opposite and *punctual* reaction, and regard the lack of one as failure. After all, we are often a reaction: Bush decides to invade Iraq; we create a global peace movement. Sometimes success looks instant: we go to Seattle and shut down the WTO, but getting to Seattle can be told as a story of months of organizing or decades of developing a movement smart enough and broad enough to understand the complex issues at hand and bring in the ten thousand blockaders. History is made out of common dreams, groundswells, turning points, watersheds—it's a landscape more complicated than commensurate cause and effect, and that peace movement came out of causes with roots reaching far beyond and long before Bush.

Effects are not proportionate to causes—not only because huge causes sometimes seem to have little effect, but because tiny ones occasionally have huge consequences. Gandhi said, "First they ignore you. Then they laugh at you. Then they fight you. Then you win." But those stages unfold slowly. As Adam Hochschild points out, it took more than three-quarters of a century to abolish slavery in Britain and the United States from the time the English Quakers first took on the issue (which slaves themselves had taken on from the beginning, of course). Only a handful of activists who began working against slavery in the late eighteenth-century beginning lived to see its mid-nineteenth-century conclusion, when what had seemed impossible suddenly began to look, in retrospect, inevitable. And as the law of unexpected activist consequences might lead you to expect, the abolition movement also sparked the first widespread women's rights movement, which took about the same amount of time to secure the right to vote for American women, and has achieved far more in the subsequent eighty-four years, and is by no means over. Activism is not a journey to the corner store, it is a plunge into the unknown. The future is always dark.

Some years ago, scientists attempted to create a long-range weather-forecasting program. It turned out that the most minute variations, even the undetectable things, the things they could perhaps not even yet imagine as data, could cause entirely different weather to emerge from almost identical initial conditions. This was famously summed up in the saying about the flap of a butterfly's wings on one continent that can change the weather on another. History is like weather, not like checkers. (And you, if you're lucky and seize the day, are like that butterfly.) Weather in its complexity, in its shifts, in the way something triggers its opposite, just as a heat wave sucks the fog off the ocean and makes my town gray and clammy after a few days of baking, weather in its moods, in its slowness, in its suddenness.

A game of checkers ends. The weather never does. That's why you can't save anything. Saving is the wrong word, one invoked over and over again, for almost every cause. Jesus saves and so do banks: they set things aside from the flux of earthly change. We never did save the whales, though we might have prevented them from becoming extinct. We will have to continue to prevent that as long as they continue not to be extinct, unless we become extinct first. That might indeed save the whales, until the sun supernovas or the species evolves into something other than whales. Saving suggests a laying up where neither moth nor rust doth corrupt; it imagines an extraction from the dangerous, unstable, ever-changing process called life on earth. But life is never so tidy and final. Only death is. Environmentalists like to say that defeats are permanent, victories temporary. Extinction, like death, is forever, but protection needs to be maintained. But now, in a world where restoration ecology is becoming increasingly important, it turns out that even defeats aren't always permanent. Across the United States, dams have been removed, wetlands and rivers restored, once-vanished native species reintroduced, endangered species regenerated.

Americans are good at responding to a crisis and then going home to let another crisis brew both because we imagine that the finality of death can be achieved in life—it's called *happily ever after* in personal life, *saved* in politics—and because we tend to think political engagement is something for emergencies rather than, as people in many other countries (and Americans at other times) have imagined it, as a part and even a pleasure of everyday life. The problem seldom goes home. Most nations agree to a ban on hunting endangered species of whale, but their ocean habitat is compromised in other ways, such as fisheries depletion and contamination. DDT is banned in the United States but exported to the developing world, and its creator, the Monsanto corporation, moves on to the next experiment.

Going home seems to be a way to abandon victories when they're still delicate, still in need of protection and encouragement. Human babies are helpless at birth, and so perhaps are victories before they've been consolidated into the culture's sense of how things should be. I wonder sometimes what would happen if victory was imagined not just as the elimination of evil but the establishment of good—if, after American slavery had been abolished, Reconstruction's promises of economic justice had been enforced by the abolitionists, or, similarly, if the end of apartheid had been seen as meaning instituting economic justice as well (or, as some South Africans put it, ending economic apartheid).

It's always too soon to go home. Most of the great victories continue to unfold, unfinished in the sense that they are not yet fully realized, but also in the sense that they continue to spread influence. A phenomenon like the civil rights movement creates a vocabulary and a toolbox for social change used around the globe, so that its effects far outstrip its goals and specific achievements—and failures. Domestically, conservatives are still fighting and co-opting it, further evidence that it's still potent. The Left likes to lash itself for its reactive politics, but on many fronts— reproductive rights, affirmative action—it's the Right that reacts, and not always successfully.

How do you map the Supreme Court's recent ruling in favor of gay rights? The conventional narrative would have it that the power rests in the hands of the nine robed ones; a more radical model would mention the gay Texas couple who chose to turn their lives inside out over many

years to press the lawsuit; and a sort of cultural ecology
would measure what made the nation rethink its homophobia, creating the societal change that the Supreme
Court only assented to: they all count. It now looks likely
that the Los Angeles River—that long, concrete ditch
through the city—will be restored over the next few dozen
years, thanks to the stubborn visionaries who believe that
even in deepest Los Angeles, a river can come back to life,
and to the changing understanding of nature that has
reached even administrators and engineers. This broad
cultural change and a few dedicated activist-catalysts may
even succeed in dismantling Glen Canyon Dam on the
Colorado River, which, by radically altering the nature of
the water flow, has been ravaging downstream ecologies
and terrains ever since. If the dam comes down, a lost
world—legendary Glen Canyon—will reappear, a river
will be reborn, and a nation will have abandoned its faith
in big technology as progress. We are not who we were not
very long ago.

11

ON THE INDIRECTNESS
OF DIRECT ACTION

A friend, Jaime Cortez, tells me I should consider the difference between hope and faith. Hope, he says, can be based on the evidence, on the track record of what might be possible—and in this book I've been trying to shift what the track record might be. But faith endures even when there's no way to imagine winning in the foreseeable future: Faith is more mystical. Jaime sees the American Left as pretty devoid of faith and connects faith to what it takes to change things in the long term, beyond what you might live to see or benefit from. I argue that what was once the Left is now so full of anomalies—of indigenous intellectuals and Catholic pacifists and the like—that maybe we do have faith—some of us.

Activism isn't reliable. It isn't fast. It isn't direct either, most of the time, even though the term *direct action* is used for that confrontation in the streets, those encounters involving lawbreaking and civil disobedience. It may be because activists move like armies through the streets that people imagine effects as direct as armies. An army assaults the physical world and takes physical possession of it; activists reclaim the streets and occasionally seize a Bastille or swarm a Berlin Wall, but the terrain of their action is usually immaterial, the realm of the symbolic, political discourse, collective imagination. They enter the conversation forcefully, but it remains a conversation. Every act is an act of faith, because you don't know what will happen. You just hope and employ whatever wisdom and experience seems most likely to get you there.

I believe all this because I've lived it, and I've lived it because I'm a writer. For twenty years I have sat alone at a desk tinkering with sentences and then sending them out, and for most of my literary life, the difference between throwing something in the trash and publishing it was imperceptible, but in the past several years the work has started coming back to me, or the readers have. Musicians and dancers face their audience and visual artists can spy on them, but reading is mostly as private as writing. Writing is lonely. It's an intimate talk with the dead, with the unborn, with the absent, with strangers, with the readers who may never come to be and who, even if they do read you, will do so weeks, years, decades later. An essay, a book, is one statement in a long conversation you could call culture or history; you are answering something or questioning something that may have fallen silent long ago, and the response to your words may come long after you're gone and never reach your ears—if anyone hears you in the first place.

After all, this is how it's been for so many books that count, books that didn't shake the world when they first appeared but blossomed later. Writing is a model for how indirect effect can be, how delayed, how invisible; no one is more hopeful than a writer, no one is a bigger gambler. Thoreau's 1849 essay "Civil Disobedience" finally found its readers in the twentieth century. (Thoreau's voice was not loud in his time, but it echoed across the continent in the 1960s and has not left us. Emily Dickinson, Walt Whitman, Walter Benjamin, and Arthur Rimbaud, like Thoreau, achieved their greatest impact long after their deaths, long after weeds had grown over the graves of most of the best sellers of their lifetimes.)

You write your books. You scatter your seeds. Rats might eat them, or they might rot. In California, some seeds lie dormant for decades because they only germinate after fire, and sometimes the burned landscape blooms most lavishly. In her book *Faith*, Sharon Salzberg recounts how she put together a collection of teachings by the Buddhist monk U Pandita and consigned the project to the "minor-good-deed category." Long afterward, she found out that while Aung San Suu Kyi, the Burmese democracy movement's leader, was isolated under house arrest by that country's dictators, the book and its instructions in meditation "became her main source of spiritual support during those intensely difficult years." Thought becomes action becomes the order of things, but no straight road takes you there.

Nobody can know the full consequences of their actions, and history is full of small acts that changed the world in surprising ways. I was one of thousands of activists at the Nevada Test Site in the late 1980s—an important, forgotten history still unfolding—out there where the United States and Great Britain have exploded more than a thousand nuclear bombs with disastrous effects on the environment and human health (and where the Bush administration would like to resume testing, thereby tearing up the last shreds of the unratified Comprehensive Test Ban Treaty). Some of the largest acts of civil disobedience in US history were committed when we walked into the place to be arrested as trespassers, thousands in a day. There, too, as in peace marches, just walking became a form of political speech, one whose directness was a delight after all the usual avenues of politicking: sitting in front of computers, going to meetings, making phone calls, dealing with money. Among the throng arrested were Quakers, Buddhists, Shoshones, Mormons, pagans, anarchists, veterans, and physicists. We would barely make the news in the United States. But we were visible on the other side of the world.

Our acts inspired the Kazakh poet Olzhas Suleimenov on February 27, 1989, to read a manifesto instead of poetry on live Kazakh TV, a manifesto demanding a shutdown of the Soviet test site in Semipalatinsk, Kazakhstan, and to call a meeting. Five thousand Kazakhs gathered at the Writer's Union the next day and formed a movement that shut down their nuclear test site. They named themselves the Nevada-Semipalatinsk Antinuclear Movement, and they acted in concert with us. "Us" by that time included the Western Shoshone, who had come to endorse our actions and point out that we and the US government were on their land; the Kazakhs identified with these indigenous people. (Someone recently called the actions at the Test Site "stale," but though we were going through old rituals of civil disobedience, in doing so we—a different "we" than before—laid a foundation for new environmental justice politics that went north to the Western Shoshone Defense Project and south to Ward Valley, where activists from the antinuclear movement and five local tribes defeated a nuclear waste dump.)

Anyway, the Soviet Test Site was shut down. The cata lyst was Suleimenov, and though we in Nevada were Suleimenov's inspiration, what gave him his platform was his poetry—in a country that loves poets. There's a wonderful parable by Jorge Luis Borges. In the last years of the thirteenth century, God tells a leopard in a cage, "You live and will die in this prison so that a man I know of may see you a certain number of times and not forget you and place your figure and symbol in a poem which has its precise place in the scheme of the universe. You suffer captivity, but you will have given a word to the poem." The poem is *The Divine Comedy*; the man who sees the leopard is Dante. Perhaps Suleimenov wrote all his poems so that one day he could stand up in front of a TV camera and deliver not a poem but a manifesto. And Arundhati Roy wrote a ravishing novel that catapulted her to international stardom, perhaps so that when she stood up to oppose dams and corporations and corruption and the destruction of the local, people would notice. Or perhaps they opposed the ravaging of the earth so that poetry too would survive in the world. A couple of years ago, a friend wrote to urge me to focus on the lyrical end of my writing rather than activism and I wrote back, "What is the purpose of resisting corporate globalization if not to protect the obscure, the ineffable, the unmarketable, the unmanageable, the local, the poetic, and the eccentric? So they need to be practiced, celebrated, and studied too, right now." I could have added that they themselves become forms of resistance; the two are not necessarily separate practices. All those years that I went to the Nevada Test Site to oppose nuclear testing, the experience was also about camping in the desert, about the beauty of the light and the grandeur of the space, about friendship and discovery. The place gave me far more than I could ever give it. Resistance is usually portrayed as a duty, but it can be a pleasure, an education, a revelation.

The year after the birth of the Nevada Semipalatinsk Movement, when some of its members were already with us at the peace camp next to the Nevada Test Site, I was the only one who attended a workshop there on Nevada and the military. The man giving it was visibly disappointed, but gave it splendidly for me alone. As we sat in the rocks and dust and creosote bush of the deep desert on a sunny day, the great Nevada organizer Bob Fulkerson taught me that the atrocities of nuclear testing were not unique in that state with a fifth of all the military land in the country, and invited me to travel into its remote reaches. He is still a cherished friend of mine and still the executive director of a coalition he founded a few years later, the Progressive Leadership Alliance of Nevada (PLAN), the most potent statewide group of its kind, bringing together environmental, labor, and human rights groups.

What came of Bob's invitation changed my life and had much to do with my book *Savage Dreams*, the first half of which is about the test site and the strands of its history wrapped around the world, and before there was the book there was an essay version of what the test site and Bob taught me that appeared in a magazine with a circulation of about half a million. A few years ago I went back to the test site for another spring action, and there I met several students from Evergreen College in Washington who had decided to come down because they had been reading

Savage Dreams in class. If you're lucky, you carry a torch
into that dark of Virginia Woolf's, and if you're really lucky
you'll sometimes see to whom you've passed it, as I did on
that day. (And if you're polite, you'll remember who handed
it to you.) I don't know if the Evergreen kids have become
great activists or died in a car crash on the way home, but I
know that for them I was a leopard prompting a word or two
of the poem of their own lives, as Bob was for me. Borges's
parable continues. On his deathbed, Dante is told by God
what the secret purpose of his life and work was. "Dante, in
wonderment, knew at last who and what he was and blessed
the bitterness of his life."

One day in Auschwitz, the writer Primo Levi recited a
canto of Dante's *Divine Comedy* to a companion, and the
poem reached out from six hundred years before to roll
back Levi's despair and his dehumanization. He lived,
and wrote marvelous books of his own, poetry after
Auschwitz in the most literal sense. American poets
became an antiwar movement themselves when Sam
Hamill declined an invitation to Laura Bush's "Poetry and
the American Voice" symposium shortly after her husband's administration announced the "Shock and Awe"
plan to saturation-bomb Baghdad. Instead, Hamill circu-
lated his letter of outrage to Ms. Bush. His e-mail inbox
filled up; he started poetsagainstthewar.org, to which
more than ten thousand poets submitted poems; and he
became a major spokesperson against the war. The poems

have been presented to governments around the world; the website has become an organizing tool for politically engaged poets, or for engaging poets politically; and an anthology of the poems—*Poets Against the War*—appeared not long after the war started.

In 1940, in his last letter to his friend Gershom Scholem, the incomparable, uncategorizable German-Jewish essayist and theorist Walter Benjamin wrote, "Every line we succeed in publishing today—no matter how uncertain the future to which we entrust it—is a victory wrenched from the powers of darkness."

12

THE ANGEL OF
ALTERNATE HISTORY

Benjamin wasn't always so optimistic. In the most celebrated passage of his "Theses on the Philosophy of History," he writes, "This is how one pictures the angel of history. His face is turned toward the past. Where we perceive a chain of events, he sees one single catastrophe which keeps piling wreckage upon wreckage and hurls it in front of his feet. The angel would like to stay, awaken the dead, and make whole what has been smashed, but a storm is blowing from Paradise; it has got caught in his wings with such violence that the angel can no longer close them." History, in Benjamin's version, is a being to whom things happen, a creature whose despairing lineaments are redeemed only by the sublimity of the imagery. It's not hard to imagine why Benjamin would picture a tragic, immobilized history, for the storm of the Third Reich was upon him when he wrote his "Theses," and it would destroy him later that year. And tragedy is seductive. After all, it is beautiful. Survival is funny. It's the former that makes the greatest art. But I want to propose another angel, a comic angel, the Angel of Alternate History.

For several years I served on the board of Nevada's statewide nonprofit environmental and antinuclear group, Citizen Alert (another consequence of meeting Bob Fulkerson). I wrote a fund-raiser for it once, modeled after *It's a Wonderful Life*. The angel in that movie, who has the pointedly unheroic name Clarence, is hapless but not paralyzed, hopeful and bumbling. Director Frank Capra's movie is a model for radical history because Clarence shows the hero what the world would look like if he hadn't been there, the only sure way to measure the effect of our acts, the one we never get. The angel Clarence's face is turned toward the futures that never come to pass. In my fund-raising letter, I described what Nevada might look like without this organization fighting the Yucca Mountain nuclear waste dump and various other atrocities visited upon the state by developers and the Departments of Defense and Energy. After all, most environmental victories look like nothing happened; the land wasn't annexed by the army, the mine didn't open, the road didn't cut through, the factory didn't spew effluents that didn't give children asthma. They are triumphs invisible except through storytelling. Citizen Alert's biggest victory is almost forgotten: the cancellation in the 1980s of the MX missile program that would've turned eastern Nevada and western Utah into a giant sacrifice area to soak up Soviet missiles in an all-out nuclear war (and paved over pristine desert to make the tracks the missiles would travel on).

Benjamin's angel tells us history is what happens, but the Angel of Alternate History tells us that our acts count, that we are making history all the time, because of what doesn't happen as well as what does. Only that angel can see the atrocities not unfolding, but we could learn to study effects more closely. Instead we don't look, and a radical change too soon becomes status quo. Young women often don't know that sexual harassment and date rape are new categories. Most forget how much more toxic rivers like the Hudson once were. Who talks about the global elimination of smallpox between 1967 and 1977? If we did more, the world would undoubtedly be better; what we have done has sometimes kept it from becoming worse.

On the west side of the Sierra Nevada is the pristine land that would have become Mineral King, a huge Disney-owned ski complex, if the Sierra Club had not fought it. On the east is Mono Lake, which has had its tributaries restored and is halfway back to historic water levels after decades of being drained by Los Angeles. The Mono Lake Committee fought from 1979 to 1996 to get the court decision that restored the lake's water and still works to protect the lake. South of there, in the Mojave Desert, near the Old Woman Mountains, is Ward Valley, which was slated for a low-level nuclear waste dump that would've likely leaked all over creation. A beautiful coalition of the five local tribes, other local people, and anti-nuclear activists fought in the deserts and the courts and with the scientific facts for ten years before defeating the dump definitively a few years ago. On the West Texas–Mexican border is the small Latino community of Sierra Blanca, where another nuclear waste dump was planned but defeated. Go east to Oklahoma and you'll arrive at the sites where, in 1993, after years of work, environmentalists—including the group Native Americans for a Clean Environment—and the Cherokee Nation shut down twenty-three percent of the world's uranium production. All these places are places of absence, or at least the absence of devastation, a few of the countless places in which there is nothing to see; nothing is what victory often looks like.

The Angel of History says, "Terrible," but this angel says, "Could be worse." They're both right, but the latter angel gives us grounds to act.

13
Viagra for Caribou

The Old Testament God rules with a heavy hand over a static moral world, but I believe that our world is instead presided over by an alternate entity, Coyote, the Native American deity, who is indestructible, lecherous, hilarious, and improvisational, straying into and surviving catastrophe (a little like his simplified great-grandson, Chuck Jones's cartoon character Wile E. Coyote). Many native creation myths do not feature a world that was perfect in the beginning, but one that was made by flawed, humorous creators who never finished the job. In that world, there was never a state of grace, never a fall, and creation continues (which is why it's ironic, or maybe comic, that white people like to situate Native Americans in the frozen diorama of Eden before the Fall). In Yahweh's world, only the good do good, and only virtue is rewarded. Coyote's world is more complicated.

It turns out, for example, that Viagra is good for endangered species. Animal parts that traditional Chinese medicine prescribed as aphrodisiacs and for treating impotence—including green turtles, seahorses, geckos, hooded and harp seals, and the velvet from the half-grown antlers of caribou—are, thanks to the new drug, no longer in such demand. What more comic form of the mysterious unfolding of the world is there than this, which suggests that Viagra's ultimate purpose may be the survival of animals at the edges of the earth? Is the erotic toil of the Viagra-saturated not selfish but performed secretly on behalf of the caribou whose antlers are no longer being cut off while they're still tender, growing like small trees with blood for sap under that velvet? The sirocco winds carry the dust of African deserts to the humid parts of Europe, and another kind of wind, as powerful and amoral as a coyote fart, carries effects from Chinese bedrooms to Arctic tundra.

And in many places, the animals are coming back. There are wolves again in Yellowstone—and, as my friend Chip Ward asks, what kind of species have we ourselves become, to restore wolves to the places where we once strove so hard to eliminate them, to yearn to see or hear these creatures we once so feared and hated? There are more buffalo on the Great Plains than at any time since the great annihilation of the 1870s, and the vision of creating "buffalo commons" hundreds or thousands of miles long may become a reality—in part because the region is losing its human population anyway. All over New England, as land that was farms in Thoreau's time and even in

Robert Frost's goes feral and gets reforested, deer, moose, bear, cougar, coyotes, and other creatures are coming back in droves. Lyme disease, named after Lyme, Connecticut, is a problem largely because deer populations have sky-rocketed and spread into suburbia—as have deer every-where, from there to the canyons of Los Angeles. It won't be the wilderness that it was—passenger pigeons will never blot out the sky again, just for starters—but it is more than anyone anticipated. Great blue herons nest in both Central and Golden Gate parks, and coyotes find their way into more and more cities. Environmental historian Richard White tells of the return of hundreds of thousands of sockeye salmon to Lake Washington in Seattle and of the enthusiasm with which people greeted them. Their return was not, he adds, the revitalization of an ancient salmon run; they were hatchery fish returning to where scientists at the University of Washington had hatched them. They were no pure ancient past coming back, but they were one version of a future with room in it for some kind of wild-ness. As White puts it, "There is a hope in that for which we might gladly surrender purity."

The Angel of Alternate History asks us to believe in the invisible; Coyote asks us to trust in the basic eccentricity of the world, its sense of humor, and its resilience. The moral worldview believes that good is accomplished through virtue, but sometimes army bases become de facto wildlife preserves; sometimes virtue falls on its face.

Sometimes Las Vegas–style casinos give Native Americans visibility and political clout. Sometimes corporations and the military demand affirmative action because it benefits them, too. Sometimes Laura Bush pushes a poet to trigger an insurrection that lets thousands of poets speak out against her husband's war.

The Internet was invented by the US military and may be one of our most valuable weapons against it, for the decentralized dissemination of information and for the organization of citizen action. The Internet can be an elitist instrument, requiring access to computers—and, usually, to electricity and phone lines—and the knowledge to use them (though a nomadic friend tells me that all through the poorest parts of the world—Thailand, Bolivia—the young flock to proliferating Internet cafés). But the Zapatista revolution was the first to make serious use of the Internet; the shutdown of the WTO meeting in Seattle was organized to a significant extent by Internet communications; and so were the 2003 antiwar actions around the world. What can be said of a medium that sometimes seems to be made half out of cheesy porn sites and yet opens these doors? Just this: Coyote pisses on moral purity and rigid definitions.

14

GETTING THE HELL
OUT OF PARADISE

erfection is a stick with which to beat the possible.
Perfectionists can find fault with anything, and no
one has higher standards in this regard than radicals. In January 2003, when Governor Ryan of Illinois
overturned 167 death sentences, reprieving everyone on
death row, there were radical commentators who found
fault with the details, carped when we should have been
pouring champagne over our heads like football champs.
But there's an increasing gap between this new movement, with its capacity for joy and carnival, and the old
figureheads. Their grumpiness is often the grumpiness of
perfectionists who hold that anything less than total victory is failure, a premise that makes it easy to give up at the
start or to disparage the victories that are possible. This is
earth. It will never be heaven. There will always be cruelty, always be violence, always be destruction. There is
tremendous devastation now. In the time it takes you to
read this book, acres of rain forest will vanish, a species
will go extinct, people will be raped, killed, dispossessed,

die of easily preventable causes. We cannot eliminate all devastation for all time, but we can reduce it, outlaw it, undermine its sources and foundations: these are victories. A better world, yes; a perfect world, never.

A million years ago I wrote a few features for the punk magazine *Maximum Rock and Roll*. One of them was about women's rights, and a cranky guy wrote in that women used to make sixty-six cents to the male dollar and that now we made seventy-seven cents, so what were we complaining about? It doesn't seem that it should be so complicated to acknowledge that seventy-seven cents is better than sixty-six cents and that seventy-seven cents isn't good enough, but the politics we have are so pathetically bipolar that we tell this story only two ways: either seventy-seven cents is a victory and victories are points where you shut up and stop fighting, or seventy-seven cents is a defeat and activism accomplishes nothing and what's the point of fighting? Both versions are defeatist because they are static. What's missing from these two ways of telling is an ability to recognize a situation in which you are traveling and have not arrived, in which you have cause both to celebrate and to fight, in which the world is always being made and is never finished. What's missing, you could say, is a sense of Coyote's world instead of Yahweh's.

In South Africa, the apartheid system was overthrown after decades of heroic struggle of every kind, but economic justice has yet to arrive; it was a seventy-seven-cent

victory. Václav Havel was a gorgeous gadfly to the communists, but as president of Czechoslovakia, then the
Czech Republic, he's been just a seventy-seven-cent
politician. "We are winning," said the graffiti in Seattle,
not "We have won." It's a way of telling in which you can
feel successful without feeling smug, in which you can
feel challenged without feeling defeated. Most victories
will be temporary, or incomplete, or compromised in
some way, and we might as well celebrate them as well as
the stunning victories that come from time to time.
Without stopping. Even if someday we get to dollar-for-
dollar parity, that will just free us up to attend to something else (just as US women's wages have advanced
compared to men's, but most working people's wages have
diminished overall since the 1970s). "Utopia is on the
horizon," declares the Uruguayan writer Eduardo
Galeano. "When I walk two steps, it takes two steps back.
I walk ten steps and it is ten steps further away. What is
utopia for? It is for this, for walking."

Judeo-Christian culture's central story is of Paradise and
the Fall. It is a story of perfection and of loss, and perhaps
a deep sense of loss is contingent upon the belief in perfection. Conservatives rear-project narratives about how
everyone used to be straight, God-fearing, decently clad,
and content with the nuclear family, narratives that any
good reading of history undoes. Activists, even those who
decry Judeo-Christian heritage as our own fall from grace,

are as prone to tell the story of paradise, though their paradise might be matriarchial or vegan or the flip side of the technological utopia of classical socialism. And they compare the possible to perfection, again and again, finding fault with the former because of the latter. Paradise is imagined as a static place, as a place before or after history, after strife and eventfulness and change: the premise is that once perfection has arrived, change is no longer necessary. This idea of perfection is also why people believe in saving, in going home, and in activism as crisis response rather than everyday practice.

Moths and other nocturnal insects navigate by the moon and stars. Those heavenly bodies are useful for them to find their way, even though they never get far from the surface of the earth. But lightbulbs and candles send them astray; they fly into the heat or the flame and die. For these creatures, to arrive is a calamity. When activists mistake heaven for some goal at which they must arrive, rather than an idea to navigate by, they burn themselves out, or they set up a totalitarian utopia in which others are burned in the flames. Don't mistake a lightbulb for the moon, and don't believe that the moon is useless unless we land on it. After all those millennia of poetry about the moon, nothing was more prosaic than the guys in space suits stomping around on the moon with their flags and golf clubs thirty-something years ago. The moon is profound *except* when we land on it.

The Czech novelist Milan Kundera said several years before his country liberated itself from Soviet-style communism, "Totalitarianism is not only hell, but also the dream of paradise—the age-old dream of a world where everybody would live in harmony, united by a single common will and faith, without secrets from each other . . . . If totalitarianism did not exploit these archetypes, which are deep inside us all and rooted deep in all religions, it could never attract so many people, especially during the early phases of its existence. Once the dream of paradise starts to turn into reality, however, here and there people begin to crop up who stand in its way, and so the rulers of paradise must build a little gulag on the side of Eden. In the course of time this gulag grows ever bigger and more perfect, while the adjoining paradise gets ever smaller and poorer . . . . It is extremely easy to condemn gulags but to reject the totalitarian poesy which leads to the gulag by way of paradise is as difficult as ever."

Paradise is not the place in which you arrive but the journey toward it. Sometimes I think victories must be temporary or incomplete; what kind of humanity would survive paradise? The United States has tried to approximate paradise in its suburbs, with *luxe, calme, volupté,* cul-de-sacs, cable television, and two-car garages, and it has produced a soft ennui that shades over into despair and a decay of the soul suggesting that paradise is already a gulag. Countless desperate teenagers will tell you so. For paradise does not require of us courage, selflessness, creativity, passion: paradise in all accounts is passive, is sedative, and if you read carefully, soulless.

That's why the poet John Keats called the world with all its suffering "this vale of soul-making," why crisis often brings out the best in us. Some imaginative Christian heretics worshipped Eve for having liberated us from paradise—the myth of the fortunate fall. The heretics recognized that before the fall we were not yet fully human—Adam and Eve need not wrestle with morality, with creation, with society, with mortality in paradise; they only realize their own potential and their own humanity in the struggle an imperfect world invites. When the Iraq war broke out, 20,000 of us in San Francisco shut down downtown, shut down streets, bridges, highways, corporations that first day and kept coming back for weeks. Out of all that conviction, all that passion, one phrase stood out for me: Gopal Dayaneni, one of the key organizers for the antiwar actions, was asked by the daily newspaper why he was getting arrested. "I have a soul," he replied.

Recent strains of activism proceed on the realization that victory is not some absolute state far away but the achieving of it, not the moon landing but the flight. A number of ideas and practices have emerged that realize this. The term "politics of prefiguration" has long been used to describe the idea that if you embody what you aspire to, you have already succeeded. That is to say, if your activism is already democratic, peaceful, creative, then in one small corner of the world these things have triumphed. Activism, in this model, is not only a toolbox to change things but a home in which to take up residence and live according to your beliefs—even if it's a temporary and local place, this paradise of participating, this vale where souls get made.

This has been an important belief for activists who recognize that change happens as much by inspiration and catalyst as by imposition. You could describe activism as having two primary strains: the attempt to change something problematic outside itself, and the attempt to build something better—though the two strains are irrevocably and necessarily intertangled, which is exactly the point of the politics of prefiguration. This idea was itself prefigured by Walter Benjamin, who wrote, "The class struggle . . . is a fight for the crude and material things without which no refined and spiritual things could exist. Nevertheless, it is not in the forms of the spoils which fall to the victor that the latter make their presence felt in the class struggle. They manifest themselves in this struggle as courage, humor, cunning, and fortitude." They are present all along the journey; arrival is at best irrelevant, at worst undermining, at least to the goods of the spirit.

Reclaim the Streets, the rowdy British movement of the later 1990s, lived this out beautifully. The premise behind

RTS's street parties seemed to be that if what they were protesting was isolation, privatization, and alienation, then a free-for-all party out in public was not just a protest but a solution, if a solution in the mode that Hakim Bey called "Temporary Autonomous Zones." (Hakim Bey contrasted these moments of liberation with revolutions proper, which "lead to the expected curve, the consensus-approved trajectory: revolution, reaction, betrayal, the founding of a stronger and even more oppressive State . . . By failing to follow this curve, the *up-rising* suggests the possibility of a movement outside and beyond the Hegelian spiral of that 'progress' which is secretly nothing more than a vicious circle.") RTS and the Anti-Roads Movement took on what could be called the post-industrialization of Britain: the privatization of everyday life and the imposition of monster roads and freeways on still-vital landscapes and communities.

There were some beautiful moments: people taking up residence in trees to which they established legal residence by receiving mail there, a tactic to keep the tree from being cut; an RTS party in which people surged onto a freeway overpass and, muffled by rave music, smuggled jackhammers onto the concrete under the giant bell-skirt of a stiltwalking grande dame, then jackhammered openings in which trees were planted. Huge street parties in downtown London linked up with activists around the world to become global anticapitalist demonstrations.

Humor, creativity, outrageousness, and exuberance were among the group's hallmarks. That RTS didn't outlive its moment was also a kind of victory, a recognition that time had moved on and the focus was elsewhere. Instead, RTS's incendiary carnival spirit, global Internet communications, and tactics of temporary victory became part of the vocabulary of what came next, the global justice movement. RTS decomposed itself into the soil from which new flowers sprang.

One day I heard a Zen Buddhist abbot from Ireland quote the Argentinian Jew Jorge Luis Borges, "There is no day without its moments of paradise." And then the day continues.

15

ACROSS THE GREAT DIVIDE

The poet and polemicist June Jordan once wrote, "We should take care so that we will lose none of the jewels of our soul. We must begin, now, to reject the white, either/or system of dividing the world into unnecessary conflict. For example, it is tragic and ridiculous to choose between Malcolm X and Dr. King: each of them hurled himself against a quite different aspect of our predicament, and both of them, literally, gave their lives to our ongoing struggle. We need everybody and all that we are." Jordan asks us to give up the dividing by which we conquer ourselves, the sectarianism, the presumption that difference is necessarily opposition. So does the activism of the moment.

That arrival of the millennium I tried to delineate could be told another way, as the departure of the binaries and oppositions by which we used to imagine the world. The end of the Soviet Bloc meant that capitalism and communism no longer defined a world of difference or a political standoff that had long been described as East versus West. The Zapatistas came along five years later with a politic that was neither capitalist nor communist, but implicitly positioned them together as means of displacing power from the individual, the community, the local. Opposition is often illusory: the old distinction between Aristotelians and Platonists, for example, overlooks how similar these two camps might be to a Taoist or a shaman. Gender, once imagined as a pair of definitive opposites, has been reimagined as a continuum of affinities and attractions.

Another binary that has become outdated is Right and Left. Though these terms are still deployed all the time, what do they define? They derive from how the French National Assembly seated itself a few years after the revolution of 1789: the more radical sat on the left, and thus radicals have been leftists ever since. Seating arrangements, however, have changed since the eighteenth century. They've changed a lot in the last fifteen years. Or perhaps we've all stood up at last and begun to move to somewhere new, somewhere unknown. The term "leftist" carries with it a baggage of socialism, utopianism, and sometimes authoritarianism that no longer delimits (and never quite did) what radicals and revolutionaries might be. Anarchists and communists can be far more different than Platonists and Aristotelians. And there are a lot of people who might embrace every item in a leftist platform except identification with the Left and its legacy.

As the Bush administration moves from what might be conventionally thought of as right-wing to something a little more totalitarian, there are dissenters on the Right who care about privacy and liberty, and occasional conservatives who actually want to conserve things. There have been strange moments before, such as Al Gore arguing for NAFTA and Ross Perot arguing against it; Arizona Republican senator John McCain fighting political corruption; animal-rights activists pursuing anti-environmental goals; feminists supporting anti-First Amendment restrictions on abortion protesters and pornography. All these suggest that there are far more than two political positions, and that the old terminology only blinds us.

I've often wondered what alliances and affinities might arise without those badges of Right and Left. For example, the recent American militia movements were patriarchial, nostalgic, nationalist, gun-happy, and full of weird fantasies about the United Nations, but they had something in common with us: they prized the local and feared its erasure by the transnational. The guys drilling with guns might've been too weird to be our allies, but they were just the frothy foam on a big wave of alienation, suspicion, and fear from people watching their livelihoods and their communities go down the tubes. What might have happened if we could have spoken directly to the people in that wave, if we could have found common ground, if we could have made our position neither Right nor Left but truly grassroots? What would have happened if we had given them an alternate version of how local power was being sapped, by whom, and what they might do about it? We need them. We need a broad base. We need a style that speaks to far more people than the Left has lately been able to speak to and for.

And without going too far into the ninety-car pileup the late sixties resembles to one who was playing with plastic horsies during that era, it does seem that the countercultural Left hijacked progressive politics and made it into something that was almost guaranteed to alienate most working people. I grew up in that Left, encouraged to despise "rednecks and white trash"—the racism of some working-class white southerners became a handy excuse for the middle class elsewhere to carry on class war while feeling progressive. Activists are still trying to shed the stereotypes the media made out of the white-radical sixties, the image in which all of us activists are spoiled, sneering, unpatriotic, and some-times violent hotheads. Of course, all activism nowadays is indebted to the other versions of what the sixties was, from the highly visible civil rights movement to the many grassroots activists who are still active.

This is part of what made Seattle so significant in 1999: the unions represented at least some rapprochement of blue-collar industrial America to environmentalists, anar-chists, indigenous activists, and farmers from Korea to

France. Farmers around the world are being ravaged by free trade, which has radicalized many of them and created new alliances, new activism, movements such as the hundred-nation coalition Via Campesino, with its hundred million members. The activist-theorist John Jordan points out that just as a wonderful coalition was born when Mexican leftists went into Chiapas and found common ground with the indigenous population, so farmer Jose Bové and his peers were revolutionaries who formed similar liaisons in the French countryside. In the American West, something similar has been happening, something that partakes of the same open-mindedness, of the best part of politics' strange bedfellows, happy in bed together, working out their differences. What gets called the Left has often had as its principal hallmark a sectarian righteousness that is also dissipating to make room for some spectacular new tactics, movements, and coalitions.

At Citizen Alert's 1996 board retreat in remote Eureka, Nevada, we all ended up drinking at the antienvironmentalist bar, because it was the only one in town with beer on tap. The purple WRANGLERS T-shirts for sale behind the bar spelled out the acronym—Western Ranchers Against No Good Leftist Environmentalist Radical Shitheads. That evening I ended up on a bar stool next to a young rancher in a large hat who thought environmentalists hated him. As it turned out, his family has been ranching in the

area for generations, he was knowledgeable about sustainable and rotational grazing—if not about the nifty new terminology for it—and boasted that his grass grazed the
bellies of his cows, unlike all the hit-and-run ranchers
nearby *he* deplored and the mining corporations he
deplored more. By the end of the evening I'd convinced
him that some environmentalists thought he might be just
fine and he was buying me Wild Turkey.

He wasn't paranoid. The Wise Use and private-property-
rights movements, like the militias, have done a much
better job of reaching out to rural communities than progressives and environmentalists have. For a long time, a
lot of environmentalists demonized ranchers. It was a
truism that cattle were ravaging the American West until
environmentalists in various places realized that sometimes ranchers were holding the line on open space:
when ranchers were forced out, development came in.
Some cattle-ranching was devastating the landscape;
some was being better managed; and new ideas about
riparian protection, rotational grazing, fire ecology, and
other rangeland management practices have been
improving the ways grazing land can be cared for.

Ranch families generally love their land and know it
with an intimacy few environmentalists will ever arrive at;
some have been there for a century and want to be there for
another one. And they, too, like farmers everywhere, are
being afflicted by price drops produced by globalization

and the industrialization of the rural (the factorylike corporate systems for producing meat, vegetables, and grains). They are a mostly unrecruited constituency of the global justice movement, in contrast to many other countries where farmers are already the backbone. In the past decade, a number of new alliances have formed in the United States, from groups like the Nature Conservancy working with ranchers to create land trusts and conservation easements to environmentalist-rancher coalitions. Widespread coalbed methane drilling in Wyoming has devastated many ranches and pushed Republican ranchers into coalition with environmentalists—as have sprawl, resort development, water crises, and the need to restore depleted land in Colorado, New Mexico, and Arizona.

Environmentalists had worked with a purist paradigm of untouched versus ravaged nature. Working with ranchers opened up the possibility of a middle way, one in which categories are porous, humans have a place in the landscape—in working landscapes, not just white-collar vacation landscapes—and activism isn't necessarily oppositional. This represents a big shift in the class politics of the once awfully white-collar environmental movement, which has been pretty good at alienating people who actually live in the environment and work with the resources in question. For the West, this means the undoing of a huge dichotomy, a huge cultural war, and a reinvention of how change works. For all of us it represents a new kind of activism, in which coalitions can be based on what wildly different groups have in common, and differences can be set aside; for a coalition requires difference as a cult does not, and sometimes it seems that the ideological litmus tests of earlier movements moved them toward cultism.

Arizona environmentalist-rancher Bill McDonald, cofounder of the Malpai Borderlands Group, may have been the one to coin the term "the radical center," the space in which ranchers, environmentalists, and government agencies have been able to work together and to see the preservation of rural livelihoods and the land itself as the same goal. The Quivera Coalition in New Mexico is the most visible example, but many small organizations around the West have been working in this center. Lynne Sherrod, who ranches near Steamboat Springs, Colorado, and heads the Colorado Cattlemen's Agricultural Land Trust, recalls, "The environmentalists and the ranchers were squared off against one another, and while we were fighting, the developers were walking off with the valley. . . . We found out we had a lot more in common than what kept us apart."

Classical environmentalism is interventionist and oppositional: it uses pressure, law, and lawsuits to prevent others from acting. The radical center, as writer and New Mexico land manager William DeBuys defines it, is "a departure from business as usual," is "not bigoted. By that

I mean that, to do this kind of work, you don't question where somebody is from or what kind of hat he or she wears, you focus on where that person is willing to go and whether he or she is willing to work constructively on matters of mutual interest. Work in the Radical Center also involves a commitment to using a diversity of tools. There is no one way of doing things. We need to have large toolboxes and to lend and borrow tools freely. Work in the Radical Center is experimental—it keeps developing new alternatives every step along the way. Nothing is ever so good that it can't stand a little revision, and nothing is ever so impossible and broken down that a try at fixing it is out of the question." It's a hopeful practice, since where litigious activism saw enemies, it sees potential allies. It's a peacemaking practice, in contrast to the warlike modes of intervention. It isn't the right answer to everything—nothing is—but it's a significant new model.

As are the legendary Ohio farmworker-organizer Baldemar Velasquez's subversive tactics. Velasquez, the founder of the Farm Labor Organizing Council, says, "Number one, I don't consider anybody opposition. I just consider anyone either misinformed or miseducated or downright wrong-thinking. That's the way I look at people, and I believe that what we do, getting justice for migrant workers, is the good and right thing in life to do and everyone ought to be on our side." Velasquez talks directly to those who might be considered "the opposition" and sometimes brings them over, a tactic that has stood him in good stead in a number of organizing battles—as have his boycotts of Campbell's Soup and other food corporations. "It's not what you serve up but how you serve it up," he told me. "The way you win people over to your side is, try to present the information from some perspective they're familiar with."

In one case, he got a lot of children of Christian Republicans in a Toledo religious school to join him by preaching to them from the Bible. An ordained minister, Velasquez "opened up the book right in front of this big assembly of high school and junior high kids, five hundred or so kids in the auditorium, and said 'let's see what God's word has to say. . . . It says that there are three groups of people God watches over jealously in the entire history of scripture, the orphans, the widows, the aliens. And how many of you want to do something about these three groups of people God watches over very jealously?' Every kid in the auditorium raised their hand. Then I asked them to do three things."

He got them to fast during lunchtime and donate their lunch money to the widow and children of a Mexican farmworker who'd died horribly in this country. He got them to educate their parents and congregations, got eight of the kids to join him in taking the money they'd raised to the family in a Nahuatl Indian village in the Mexican mountains where they saw firsthand the poverty that sends immigrants to the United States. And then he got more than three hundred of these children of conservative Christians to join him in a protest of the supermarkets selling the pickles that were the subject of a farmworkers' battle. He won that battle, too, prompting many supermarkets to stop carrying the brand, thereby forcing the pickle growers to keep the crop in Ohio and to treat farmworkers as employees rather than sharecroppers. He's worked with international labor issues, with environmental justice issues, with the larger networks within which farmworkers toil. But what makes him remarkable is not just this making of connections between issues, but between sides.

I n important ways, these little ripples of inspired
activism around the United States parallel aspects of
the global justice movement and the Zapatistas. All
three share an improvisational, collaborative, creative
process that is in profound ways anti-ideological, if ideology means ironclad preconceptions about who's an ally
and how to make a better future. There's an openhearted-
ness, a hopefulness, and a willingness to change and to
trust. Cornel West came up with the idea of the jazz
freedom fighter and defined jazz "not so much as a term
for a musical art form but for a mode of being in the
world, an improvisational mode of protean, fluid and flex-
ible disposition toward reality suspicious of 'either/or'
viewpoints." That similar journeys beyond binary logic and
rigid ideology should be happening in such different arenas
suggests that when we talk about a movement we are not
talking about a specific population or a specific agenda but
a zeitgeist, a change in the air.

Or perhaps we should not talk about a movement, or
movements, but about *movement*: to apprehend these wild

changes is as though to see many, many groups of people get up and move around from the positions they sat in for so long. Charles Derber calls this the "third wave," claiming it as a successor to the first wave of 1960s-style activism and the second wave of fragmented identity politics: "While the third wave has begun serious new political thinking about global alternatives, it is basically antidoctrinal, in contrast to both the first and second waves. This reflects the huge variety of global constituencies and the need to accommodate their many issues and points of view. Resisting a 'party line' has kept the movement together." To be antidoctrinal is to open yourself up to new and unexpected alliances, to new networks of power. It's to reject the static utopia in favor of the improvisational journey. Just as the environmental movement is the beneficiary of an enormously more sophisticated understanding of natural systems, so activism benefits from the mistakes, inspirations, and tools provided by past movements.

Naomi Klein remarked about global justice activists a few years ago, "When critics say the protesters lack vision, what they are really saying is that they lack an overarching revolutionary philosophy—like Marxism, democratic socialism, deep ecology or social anarchy—on which they all agree. That is absolutely true, and for this we should be extraordinarily thankful. At the moment, the anti-corporate street activists are ringed by would-be leaders, anxious to enlist them as foot soldiers for their particular cause. It is to this young movement's credit that it has as yet fended off all of these agendas and has rejected everyone's generously donated manifesto." Elsewhere she described Marcos and the Zapatistas in terms that exactly fit the loose networks of anarchist antiglobalization activists: "non-hierarchical decision-making, decentralized organizing, and deep community democracy." This is an ideology of sorts, but an ideology of absolute democracy that's about preventing authority from rising, with the concomitant limits on imagination, participation, adaptation, which is to say that it is an ideology against ideologies. If there were purist or Puritan tendencies in earlier waves of activism, this is generously, joyously impure, with the impurity that comes from mixing and circulating and stirring things up.

From deep inside that community, my friend John Jordan, a wonderful writer and activist—part of Reclaim the Streets then, of the global justice movement now—writes me, "Our movements are trying to create a politics that challenges all the certainties of traditional leftist politics, not by replacing them with new ones, but by dissolving any notion that we have answers, plans or strategies that are watertight or universal. In fact our strategies must be more like water itself, undermining everything that is fixed, hard and rigid with fluidity, constant movement and evolution. We are trying to build a politics of process, where the only certainty is doing what feels right at the right time and in the right place—a politics that doesn't wait (interesting how wait and hope are the same words in Spanish) but acts in the moment, not to create something in the future but to build in the present, it's the politics of the here and now. When we are asked how are we going to build a new world, our answer is, 'We don't know, but let's build it together.' In effect we are saying the end is not as important as the means, we are turning hundreds of years of political form and content on its head by putting the means before the ends, by putting context in front of ideology, by rejecting purity and perfection, in fact, we are turning our backs on the future.

"It's an enormous challenge, because in a chaotic world people need something to hold onto and something to hold them, if all is uncertain, if uncertainty is the only certainty, then the uprooted, the fragile, those that crave something to give them meaning in their lives, simply get washed away by the flood and flux of an unsure universe. For them, hope is often found in certainty. Not necessarily certainty rooted in a predictable future, but certainty that they are doing the right thing with their lives . . . . Taking power has been the goal at the end of the very straight and narrow road of most political movements of the past. Taking control of the future lies at the root of nearly every historical social change strategy, and yet we are building movements which believe that to 'let go' is the most powerful thing we can do—to let go, walk away from power and find freedom. Giving people back their creative agency, reactivating their potential for a direct intervention into the world is at the heart of the process. With agency and meaning reclaimed, perhaps it is possible to imagine tomorrow today and to be wary of desires that can only be fulfilled by the future. In that moment of creation, the need for certainty is subsumed by the joy of doing, and the doing is filled with meaning."

Jordan's vision is widely shared. The philosopher Alphonso Lingis says, "We really have to free the notion of liberation and revolution from the idea of permanently setting up some other kind of society." Subcommandante Marcos understands well that what older revolutionary movements would have considered victory would be defeat for the Zapatistas, and he calls Zapatismo "not an ideology but an intuition." Zapatista scholar John Holloway has a new manifesto of a book out called *Change the World without Taking Power*, a similar argument that the revolution is an end in itself that fails its spirit and its ideals when it becomes the next institutional power. Or as my brother David, a global justice organizer, writes, "The notion of capturing positions of power, either through elections or insurrection, misses the point that the aim of revolution is to fundamentally change the relations of power. There is a vast area of do-it-yourself activity directed toward changing the world that does not have the state as its focus and that does not aim at gaining positions of power. It is an arena in which the old distinctions between reform and revolution no longer seem relevant, simply because the question of who controls the state is not the focus of attention." This is what the Temporary Autonomous Zones, the politics of prefiguration, the adage about process, not product, have all been inching toward—a revolution in the nature of revolution, with the promise that whatever mistakes we make, they will not be the same old ones.

Sandinista poet Giaconda Belli writes that July 18 and 19, 1979, when the Sandinista rebels overthrew the Somoza dictatorship in Nicaragua, were "two days that felt as if a magical, age-old spell had been cast over us, taking us back to Genesis, to the very site of the creation of the world." These other versions of what revolution means suggest that the goal is not so much to go on and create the world as to live in that time of creation, and with this the emphasis shifts from institutional power to the power of consciousness and the enactments of daily life. Revolutionary moments have an extraordinary intensity, the intensity of living in history, of feeling the power to make one's life and make the world, the communion between people liberated from the bonds that limit and separate them. "Revolutionary moments are carnivals in which the individual life celebrates its unification with a regenerated society," writes Situationist Raoul Vaneigem.

The question, then, is not so much how to create the world as how to keep alive that moment of creation, how to realize that Coyote world in which creation never ends and people participate in the power of being creators, a world whose hopefulness lies in its unfinishedness, its openness to improvisation and participation. The revolutionary days I have been outlining are days in which hope is no longer fixed on the future: it becomes an electrifying force in the present.

17

THE GLOBAL LOCAL

A decade or so ago I was repeating to my aunt the then-current critique of the 1955 exhibition and book *The Family of Man*. It was popular to denigrate it for its insistence on a universal humanity painted in the broadest terms, its photographs suggesting that motherhood or voting or work was ultimately the same everywhere, in disregard of the differences that postmodernism and multiculturalism have emphasized. My aunt exclaimed, "You don't understand what it was like then, how divided we were, how important it was to find common ground after the war and the holocaust and against the racism that was still rampant." The recent focus on difference and the local of late has been a counterbalance not only to the universalizing "truths" of modernism but to the homogenizing, power-consolidating forces of corporate culture and agriculture.

But the political commentator Danny Postel writes, "As the Egyptian sociologist and dissident Saad Eddin Ibrahim has noted, when human rights activists from different countries get together and exchange notes, they invariably find that, despite wide geographic, cultural and religious chasms, they share many of the same experiences and speak a remarkably common idiom." The answer to most either/or questions is "both"; the best response to a paradox is to embrace both sides instead of cutting off one or the other for the sake of coherence. The question is about negotiating a viable relationship between the local and the global, not signing up with one and shutting out the other.

One way to define the global justice movement of our time is as a global movement in defense of the local—of local food, local jurisdiction over labor and resources, local production, local culture, local species, domesticated and wild, of the protection of environments that are by definition local. The old slogan that went "Think globally, act locally" could be stood on its head as "Think locally, act globally," for the local is one way to describe what's under assault by transnational corporations but the resistance is often globally networked. Much of the radicalism of our time is in celebration and defense of the local—but it would be too simple to set up the local as the good. Think of how the civil rights movement appealed to the federal government to dismantle the South's local customs of apartheid, intimidation, and voter exclusion or, nowadays, of the many westerners who resent the federal government for interfering with their perceived right to assault the local environment for fun and profit. Sometimes broader forces counteract a malignant local.

In the period my aunt spoke of, a racialist-nationalist localism had devastated the world. In our time, a lot of the devastation is wrought by and for transnational capital, to which the local serves as a counterbalance. The local can mean human scale, a scale on which people can be heard, make a difference, understand the dynamics of power and hold it accountable. In the 1970s, mostly in rural places, mostly on the West Coast, some attempted to return to and to rethink the local (which other cultures had never left), in the movement or tendency called bioregionalism. It was an attempt to live within the potential meanings, communities, limitations, and long-term prospects of a region, to live on local terms, eat local foods, to know exactly where you were and how to take care of it. It was about belonging to a place not as a birthright but as an act of conscious engagement. In some ways bioregionalism prefigures the anti-ideological of the present in that it was about adapting rather than imposing, and its emphasis on the local meant that it wasn't preaching a gospel that could be exported without alteration. Imposition is about consolidation of power; the local I'm interested in is about dispersing it.

A dozen years ago, the environmental writer and trickster Jim Dodge remarked, "I'm not so sure bioregionalism even has a doctrine to be pure about — it's more a sense of direction (uphill, it seems) than the usual leftist highway to Utopia . . . ." Bioregionalism was an attempt to return to what human life had been for most of history, ecologically and socially, to return not nostalgically but radically, with a sense that this could also be the future, that it was the only viable future. Though you don't hear much about bioregionalism anymore, its ideals are present in the slow food movement, the farmers' markets springing up everywhere in the United States and Britain, the emphases on eating locally and seasonally, environmentally sound building practices, sustainable urban designs and systems for garbage, water, and power, and in the revivals that celebrate and maintain local culture and memory amid the homogenization that is corporate globalization's cultural impact.

Dodge claims anarchy as an essential element of bioregionalism, "the conviction that we as a community, or a tight, small-scale federation of communities, can mind our own business, and can make decisions regarding our individual and communal lives and gladly accept the responsibilities and consequences of those decisions." This brings us back to the activism of the past twenty years. Or more, since contemporary anarchist organizing draws upon the decentralized models of the anarchists of the Spanish Civil War for its affinity groups—the more or less autonomous associations of five to fifteen people that constitute the basic unit of direct action. Eddie Yuen, defining the activists in Seattle in 1999, spoke of "commitment to direct democracy, as specifically the organizational forms of the affinity group, decentralized spokes-council meetings and consensus process."

In other words, they were, or rather we are, anarchists, and this mode of organizing comes most directly out of the antinuclear movement of the 1980s, where direct democracy was established through affinity groups and spokescouncils using consensus decision-making processes (a spokescouncil is a meeting to which member affinity groups have each sent a spokesperson). Anarchy is an incendiary word that might be better set aside, not least since it comes from a Eurocentric history that doesn't encompass, for example, traditional participatory cultures, which are equally important as sources and presences, and in which membership in the community counterbalances and channels the rights of individuals. Another way to describe a lot of this nameless movement is as a resurgence of antihierarchical direct democracy—the dispersal or localization of power. In Argentina, which since December 2001 has had a severe economic crisis and an inspired rise of neighborhood and community groups to replace failed institutions, it's called horizontality. Perhaps it's all just democracy at its most potent.

The embrace of local power doesn't have to mean parochialism, withdrawal, or intolerance, only a coherent foundation from which to navigate the larger world. From the wild coalitions of the global justice movement to the cowboys and environmentalists sitting down together, there is an ease with difference that doesn't need to be eliminated, a sense that if the essentials of the principle or goal are powerful enough you can work together, and that perhaps differences are a strength, not a weakness. A sense that you can have an identity embedded in local circumstance and a role in the global dialogue. And that this global dialogue exists in service of the local. The Maori of New Zealand have had significant success in reviving their language, and Native Hawaiians have modeled their language programs after the Maori and in turn become models for the wave of language preservations and promulgations across Native North America. So this other globalization, the globalization of communication and of ideas, can be the antithesis of the homogenization and consolidation brought by the spread of chains and brands and corporations. It can be the small in opposition to the big: Arundhati Roy writes of "the dismantling of the Big—big bombs, big dams, big ideologies, big contradictions, big heroes, big mistakes. Perhaps it will be the Century of the Small."

The best way to resist a monolithic institution or corporation is not with a monolithic movement but with multiplicity itself. Of course the big story is Fox News in the United States, Rupert Murdoch's empire in the English-speaking world, Prime Minister Berlusconi's media monopoly in Italy, the great consolidations—but the little stories are a hundred thousand websites, listserves, and blogs on the net, the hundreds of Indymedia sites around the world launched in kinship with the Seattle 1999 mothersite, and so forth. The counter to Monsanto corporation's genetic engineering and agricultural patents isn't just anti-G.M. (genetically modified) and anti-patenting activism and legislation, it's local farmers, farmers' markets, seed diversity, organic crops, integrated pest management, and other practices that work best on the small scale. A farmers' market selling the produce of local farmers isn't an adequate solution, but ten thousand of them begin to be. This creates alternatives that are far less visible and individually far less powerful; domination by Monsanto is news in a way that the arrival of the first chiles or peaches at the farmers' market is not (though, as I write, citizen pressure and mounting scientific evidence have caused Monsanto to shut down its European branch, and citizen outcry in the United States caused its genetically engineered New Leaf potato to go out of production).

For a long time, I've thought that the purpose of activism and art, or at least of mine, is to make a world in which people are producers of meaning, not consumers, and writing this book I now see how this is connected to the politics of hope and to those revolutionary days that are the days of the creation of the world. Decentralization and direct democracy could, in one definition, be this politic in which people are producers, possessed of power and vision, in an unfinished world.

18

INTERRUPTION:
THE WORLD CATCHES FIRE

It's September 2003. I'm writing a book on hope. I'm having a really harrowing week. At the end of it, what seems another of the great labor pangs in the birth of a new millennium happens, a glorious moment of another world becoming possible, becoming present, becoming ours. Walls come down. Farmers rise up. Global power shifts. But the news hardly reaches the United States, and only a few insiders go ecstatic.

This is the week the third World Trade Organization ministerial is held in the tourist-resort town of Cancún, Mexico. Before it began, we expected that the talks would falter. The United States and the European Union were pressuring the impoverished countries to surrender more autonomy without giving them any reward and without being willing to address the way agricultural subsidies in the developed world ravage farming in the less developed one. But thanks to an unanticipated solidarity between activists, non-governmental organizations, and impoverished nations, the WTO talks didn't just falter; they collapsed spectacularly. An activist, Antonio Juhasz, e-mailed us, "A woman from Swaziland turned to a colleague of mine and told him that the African countries could not have stood firm against the WTO, the US and the EU if had not been for the activists in and outside of the convention hall. She said that our actions in and outside, our words, our pressure — particularly as they reached the press— gave her and her fellow African nations the strength to take this historic stand." Another activist says that it was the presence of the farmers outside that pressured the nations inside to stand up, to remember whose lives were at stake, that kept Korea, for example, where one out of six families is a farm family, from bargaining away more of its local agriculture.

At the Cancún ministerial, the impoverished nations created a coalition called the Group of Twenty-plus that represents nearly half the world's people and more than two-thirds of its farmers, a group powerful enough to stand up to the rich nations and the corporations they represent. The coalition (in which India, China, and many smaller nations don't have to reconcile their differences) was assembled by Brazil, which, under the leadership of Luiz Inacio "Lula" da Silva, is a beautiful maverick. At 3 P.M. on the last day of the meeting, the Kenyan delegate said, "This meeting is over. This is another Seattle," and with that the Group of Twenty-plus walked and the talks collapsed. The non-governmental organization members present went wild with joy and the demonstrators outside began to celebrate. British *Guardian* commentator George Monbiot wrote, "At Cancún the weak nations stood up to the most powerful negotiators on earth and were not broken. The lesson they will bring home is that if this is possible, almost anything is."

It was a triumph for farmers, for the poor, for the power of nonviolent direct action, for the power of people over corporations and justice over greed. It was a power shift, both from the rich nations to the poor and from the towers to the streets. Seattle was led by young white radicals, though representatives of all the world were there, but Cancún was led by Mexican *campesinos* and Korean farmers representing huge constituencies (including seventy nations and the hundred million members of the groups in the Via Campesino coalition), which gave it a different tone and a different authority. They were able to speak for the world as we were not. And they demonstrated how broad-based the movement was, how meaningful the common ground attained by such different players. Unfolding as it did on the second anniversary of 9/11, the revolution in Cancún reclaimed some of the peaceful populist power that Osama bin Laden and Bush had paralyzed. Once the WTO looked unstoppable; now its survival has been thrown into doubt.

At the beginning of the week of actions, about seven thousand activists marched to one of the many barricades set up to keep them away from the WTO meeting—one of the ironies of the WTO and other global institutions of power is that their rhetoric of open borders can only be issued from behind policed barricades. Lee Kyung-hae, a farmer who had, like thousands of Korean farmers, been bankrupted by free trade and become a passionate activist for farmers' survival, arrived with his contingent. He wore a sandwich board saying "The WTO kills farmers" and climbed to the top of the fence, where he stabbed himself in the heart. Later that day he died. His self-immolation created a somber, respectful mood, a sense of united purpose, a moral authority and an urgency that shaped the actions for the days to come, and he was commemorated in countless ways. His death, by all accounts, opened the way to victory.

The last great action of the week made visible what had been achieved. As Peter Rosset of Food First tells it, "Everyone feared the worst sort of confrontation on Saturday, and the police brought in massive reinforcements. They tripled the size of the metal barriers, and the provocateurs showed up in greater numbers, with shopping carts filled with stones and huge metal bars. But the diverse sectors of legitimate protestors came together in an amazing plan that produced the most beautiful, moving and symbolic protest imaginable, so powerful that we were all sure we had reached and passed the turning point vis-à-vis the WTO."

The black block—black-clad kids with bandannas over

their faces and a reputation for property destruction—had
been asked by the Mexicans to provide security, and so
this group sometimes at odds with the rest of the demonstrators became their guards against the paid provocateurs. A hundred women of all kinds—young and old,
indigenous, European, African—went forward with bolt
cutters and cut the fence free. Korean farmers attached
long ropes, and thousands of people pulled down the
walls. On the other side stood police ready for a confrontation, but the Koreans on the front line turned their
backs on them and began a mass memorial for Mr. Lee.
Everyone sat down. People sang. The WTO was burnt in
effigy. And the activists left without confrontation, having
defined the space and the action themselves. The police
were stunned and the hundreds of journalists marveled at,
as Rosset says, "our collective ability to do the unexpected,
to turn promised violence into moving peace, and to
make a statement so powerful that the WTO could not
hope to resist."

A month or two before the Bush administration began
bombing Baghdad, several months before this victory in
Cancún, Jonathan Schell published *The Unconquerable
World: Power, Nonviolence, and the Will of the People*. The
book eloquently argues for a new idea of change and of
power. One of its key recognitions is that the change that
counts in revolution takes place first in the imagination.

Histories usually pick up when the action begins, but Schell quotes John Adams saying that the American Revolution "was in the minds of the people, and in the union of the colonies, both of which were accomplished before hostilities commenced." And Thomas Jefferson concluded, "This was effected from 1760 to 1775, in the course of fifteen years, before a drop of blood was shed at Lexington."

This means, of course, that the most foundational change of all, the one from which all else issues, is hardest to track. It means that politics arise out of culture, out of the spread of ideas and the shaping of imaginations. It means that symbolic and cultural acts have real political power. Schell describes how the United States lost the war in Vietnam because, despite extraordinary military superiority, it could not win over the people of that country and finally lost the confidence and support of its own citizens: "In the new world of politically committed and active people, it was not force per se but the collective wills of those peoples that were decisive." In other words, belief can be more effective than violence. Nonviolent action, Schell argues, has in the last century become an increasingly powerful force in the world, a counterforce to war and to violence. This claim was mocked during the opening salvos of the Iraq war, but the quagmire of that war and the opposition to it around the world have strengthened his case. It's an immensely hopeful position, identifying the rise of nonviolence and the importance of its role in times and places where few had noticed it, as well as in those—Gandhi's India, King's South—where we had. It is a reminder of our power to make the world.

Schell continues, "Individual hearts and minds change; those who have been changed become aware of one another; still others are emboldened, in a contagion of boldness; the 'impossible' becomes possible; immediately it is done, surprising the actors almost as much as their opponents; and suddenly, almost with the swiftness of thought—whose transformation has in fact set the whole process in motion—the old regime, a moment ago so impressive, vanishes like a mirage." Cancún 2003, where the power of small-scale farmers and other activists proved supreme and the apparently inexorable advance of the WTO was halted and turned back, was one of those carnival moments of hope realized, one of the days of creation.

19

A Dream Three Times
the Size of Texas

I have long been fascinated by October 12, 1992, the five-hundredth anniversary of Christopher Columbus's arrival in the Americas. Just as Laura Bush's attempt to hold a poetry seminar turned into a poets' outcry against her husband's war, so the plan to celebrate the Columbian Quincentennial was overwhelmed by opposition to that celebration of colonialism. Indigenous people throughout the western hemisphere used the occasion—not just a single day, but a discussion that began long before and continues yet—to assert their own history of the Americas, as a place that was not discovered but invaded. Invaded but not quite conquered, for though much was lost, the quincentennial was an occasion for many native groups to assert that they are still here, that they remember, and that this history is not over.

Thus the quincentennial became an occasion for many nonnatives to relearn the genocidal history of the Americas and sometimes address those parts of the history still with us—questions of sovereignty, visibility, representation, reparation, and land rights, among other things. Thus, remembering the past became the grounds to make change in the present. Thus, culture becomes politics. In the end, the day did not commemorate the start of an era but marked in some subtle way the beginning of its end. Perhaps I should have counted October 12, 1992 as one of the key moments of the millennium—except that what mattered most didn't happen just on that day, but all around it.

After the Second World War, one of the programs to dissolve Native Americans' identity, diffuse their power, and detach them from their land base involved resettling them in the cities to assimilate. For many, cities instead gave them access to new resources and information and fostered intertribal political alliances. Out of this, in Minneapolis, came the American Indian Movement, AIM, in 1968 (and, of course, out of the hope for justice and tactics for achieving it offered by the civil rights movement and out of the carnival of the later 1960s). Out of an AIM conference in 1974 came the International Indian Treaty Council. In 1977, the Treaty Council went to the United Nations, where it became the first indigenous organization to apply for and receive non-governmental organization—NGO—status. So you can trace the quincentennial back to 1974, or 1968, or, for that matter 1492, along a zigzag trail of encounters, reactions, and realizations.

Treaty Council activist Roxanne Dunbar-Ortiz was at

the UN General Assembly in 1980 when Spain proposed that 1992 be declared the "year of encounter of civilizations" and "it was the most amazing thing—every African government representative stood up and walked out, so I walked out. They were not thinking about indigenous people, but this was the onset of slavery and they sure knew that." South Africa's African National Congress and African NGOs would prove important allies for the UN-based struggle for indigenous rights. Spain had planted the idea of the quincentennial of Columbus's arrival, but indigenous-rights activists would reshape it into an antithesis of Spain's agenda.

"We never got one single line of media attention," says Dunbar-Ortiz of the early years. Getting the word out was "just really hard work" carried out by speakers traveling to reservations, groups, and conferences, and by publishing a newsletter put together by the poet Simon Ortiz, among others. Word spread, and ideas began to shift. Dunbar-Ortiz told me, "It is exactly what gives you hope when you see this happen—when you see how hungry people are for the truth. When it is offered to them, they seize it." Truth has been at least as important as law in the shift of status of indigenous Americans, for even the legal gains seem to be built on a foundation of changed imagination and rewritten history. Columbus Day became an occasion to rethink the past, and rethinking the past opened the way to a different future.

Nonindigenous Americans often embraced two contra-
dictory, not-so-true stories before that change. One was that
Native Americans had all been wiped out—the tale of how
a frail, static people had been swept away by progress was
sometimes told sadly, but seldom questioned. Even radicals seemed in love with this tragedy, and again and again
books casually assert some tribe or nation has vanished that
hasn't. We had the end of the trail, the last of the Mohicans,
a vanishing race, a dying nation, a doomed people, stories
that might condemn the past but let us off the hook for unfinished conflicts. In the other key story, there never had been
any Native Americans, because the continent had been pristine, untouched, virgin wilderness before we got here, a story
particularly dear to environmentalists who saw nature as a
nonhuman realm, a place apart. Putting Native Americans
back in the picture meant radically redefining what nature
means and what the human place in it might be (another
undoing of a dichotomy, the nature-culture divide, with profound implications for the environmental movement,
which has not yet altogether come to terms with this revision of meaning). Putting them in the present meant that
the Indian wars are not over. The difference is that in recent
years they have begun to win, some things, some of the time,
and that this time the wars are mostly in the courts, in
Congress, over textbooks, novels, movies, monuments,
museums, and mascots, as well as on and over the land.

The quincentennial became an opportunity to restate

what Columbus's arrival had meant—invasion, colonialism, genocide—and what it had been met with—"500
years of resistance" was the catchphrase. Other factors,
from academic discourse to the legal ruling that made
Native American casinos pop up across the country (you
can't lose your shirt to an extinct people), shifted the terms
of Native American visibility and historical memory. But
it was the quincentennial that had made the Zapatistas say
"*basta*," enough, and decide to emerge from hiding fifteen
months later. And it was probably the quincentennial conversation, as well as the brutal civil war in Guatemala, that
moved the Nobel Committee to give the Nobel Peace
Prize to indigenous Guatemalan human rights activist
Rigoberta Menchu.

Since then, a surge of indigenous power has transformed the face of politics in many Latin American states,
including Colombia, Ecuador, Peru, and Bolivia. For
example, in 2000, Ecuadoran general Lucio Gutierrez
was ordered to repress protests against government policy
by tens of thousands of indigenous Ecuadorans. Instead,
he set up kitchens to feed them, permitted them to
occupy the Congress, and joined an indigenous leader in
announcing a new government. He was jailed for this disobedience, kicked out of the army—and in 2002 he was
elected president, the first time indigenous people had
exercised such power anywhere in the hemisphere. Far
from perfect, he still represents a crucial shift in power.

Gutierrez was elected one month after the 510th anniversary of Columbus's arrival, which became another day of hemispheric action stretching from Canada to Chile, ten months before the victory in Cancún led in part by indigenous Yucatán farmers. In the United States, the gains have been on many fronts, from the repatriation of indigenous corpses and skeletons in museum collections to lawsuits against the Department of the Interior for "losing" billions of dollars that belong to the tribes, along with the records of that money. The number of people identifying as Native American more than doubled between the 1990 and 2000 censuses, in part because the new census recognized mixed-race identities, but also because far more people were willing to acknowledge an identity that had once been denigrated. From being a dying race, the indigenous peoples of the Americas have become a growing force.

The Coast Miwok were supposed to be extinct when I was growing up on their territory; in 1992 they began fighting for federal recognition, and in 2000, led by the gifted part-Miwok novelist Greg Sarris, they got it. In Yosemite National Park, the cradle of the concept of virgin nature, the native people who were wiped out of the official representations—park signage, park histories, land-management policies—have in the past decade reappeared in those contested cultural sites. And they've won the right to build their own cultural center in the park, a small victory for them but a big shift in defining what nature might mean and who will define it for the four million visitors per year. The Timbisha Shoshone, whose homeland became Death Valley National Park, have won far more. In 1994 they won federal recognition of their status as a tribe with unextinguished rights, and in 2000 they gained jurisdiction over nearly eight thousand acres in the park, as well as extensive lands outside the park.

And this scale is dwarfed by other victories. The Inuit activist John Amagoalik remembers that in the 1960s journalists would come to his Arctic homeland and write about it as "a wasteland where nobody lives . . . There was always agreement between them that Inuit could not survive as a people. They all agreed that Inuit culture and language 'will disappear.' " On April 1, 1999, the Inuit got their homeland back. They won from the Canadian government their own autonomously governed province, Nunavut, a huge tract of far northeastern land three times the size of Texas, ten times the size of Britain, a fifth of all Canada.

How do you measure the space between a shift in cultural conversation and a landmass three times the size of Texas? What bridges the space between that hope and that realization? What is the scale of the imagination and of the will? What sustained the people whose uncountable small acts shifted the world, since almost no such act has a reward in itself, or soon, or certainly? From what vantage point can you see such incremental, such incomplete, but such extraordinary transformation?

The resurgence of the indigenous peoples of the Americas means many things. One is that there are usually cracks somewhere in the inevitable and the obvious. Another is that capitalism and state socialism do not define the range of possibilities, for the indigenous nations often represent significantly different ways of imagining and administrating social and economic systems as well as of connecting spirituality to politics. Relegated to history's graveyard, they have, as the Zapatistas did, inspired the birth of another future. "Another world is possible" has become a rallying cry, and in some ways this is their world, the other future drawn from another past recovered despite everything. This resurgence also demonstrates the sidelong ways of change: from an argument in Geneva to a landmass in northern Canada, from a critique of the past to a new path into the future, from ideas and words to land and power. This is how history is made, out of such unlikely materials, and of hope.

B ut the ice on Ellesmere Island at the heart of
Nunavut is melting and polar bears are in trouble,
for their hunting is dependent on summer ice,
and chemical contamination is turning some of them into
hermaphrodites. There are no words in the native languages for the new birds arriving in the warming far north.
Chunks of the Antarctic ice shelf the size of small New
England states are falling into the sea, which is rising
enough to threaten the very existence of some of the small
islands in the world and the cultures of those islands.
Global warming is killing far more people than terrorism.
There are nightmarish things at large, and it is not my
purpose to deny them. What are the grounds of hope in
this world of wrecks?

The United States is the most disproportionate pro-
ducer of global warming, governed by the most disre-
gardful administration. This country often seems like a
train heading for a crash, with a gullible, apolitical, easily
distracted population bloating itself on television's political

distortions and repellent vision of human life, runaway
rates of consumption, violent interventions around the
world, burgeoning prison and impoverished and crazy
populations, the malignancy of domestic fundamen-
talism, the decay of democracy, and on and on. It's hard
to see radical change in the United States, and easy to see
how necessary it is. I spend a lot of time looking at my
country in horror.

And a lot of time saying *but* . . . But some plants die
from the center and grow outward. The official United
States seems like the rotten center of a flourishing world,
for elsewhere, particularly around the edges, and even in
the margins of this country, beautiful insurrections are
flowering. American electoral politics is not the most
hopeful direction to look in, and yet the very disastrous-
ness seems sometimes to offer possibility. The Bush
administration seems to be doing what every previous
administration was too prudent to do: pursuing its unen-
lightened self-interest so recklessly that it is undermining
US standing in the world and the economy that under-
wrote that standing. The great peace march of February
15, 2003 was a sort of global "fuck you" to that administration, as was the UN Security Council's refusal to endorse
the war in Iraq a month later, as was the resistance in
Cancún (and at the next staging ground for the US government's globalization agenda, the November 2003 Free
Trade Area of the Americas conference in Miami, where

the agreements were all postponed or defanged). This won't yield any rapid results, but like polar ice, the old alignments are falling apart, and this time the breakup is liberatory, a birth into the utter unknown of a brave new world.

And this very unknown gives me hope. "The future is dark, which is on the whole, the best thing the future can be, I think," said Virginia Woolf in the midst of the First World War, a war in which millions of young men died horribly. They died, but not everything did. Woolf committed suicide during the next war, but before that she created a body of work of extraordinary beauty and power, power put to use by women to liberate themselves in the years after Woolf was gone, beauty still setting minds on fire.

For many years, one of the great annual sources of gloom has been the Worldwatch Institute's *State of the World* report, but the 2003 report strikes some startling notes. In it, the aptly named Chris Bright writes, "But the biggest obstacle to reinventing ourselves may be simply a kind of paralysis of hope. It is possible to see very clearly that our current economies are toxic, destructive on a gargantuan scale, and grossly unfair—to see all this and still have difficulty imagining effective reform. . . . We are used to constant flux in the daily details of existence, yet the basic structure of the status quo always looks so unalterable. But it's not. Profound change for the better does occur, even though it can be difficult to see because one of the most common effects of success is to be taken for granted. What looks perfectly ordinary after the fact would often have seemed like a miracle before it."

I have been outlining a series of extraordinary changes in my lifetime, changes that have realized radically different lives for some of us and consciousness for most of us. Or, in Bright's terms, miracles. And I have tried to outline this vast, inchoate, nameless movement — not a political movement but a global restlessness, a pervasive shift of imagination and desire — that has recently appeared in almost every part of the world. This, I think, has only just begun, and though it has achieved countless small-scale victories around the world, what its creativity and its power will achieve is yet unimaginable. I have harped on the global justice movement, but there are many other phenomena — for example, South Africa's Truth and Reconciliation Commission, as an evolution beyond the binary of vengeance versus acquiescence or silence, a model that is being followed elsewhere. An extraordinary imaginative power to reinvent ourselves is at large in the world, though it is hard to say how it will counteract the dead weight of neoliberalism, fundamentalisms, environmental destructions, and well-marketed mindlessness.

But hope is not about what we expect. It is an embrace of the essential unknowability of the world, of the breaks with the present, the surprises. Or perhaps studying the record more carefully leads us to expect miracles — not when and where we expect them, but to expect to be astonished, to expect that we don't know. And this is grounds to act. I believe in hope as an act of defiance, or rather as the foundation for an ongoing series of acts of defiance, those acts necessary to bring about some of what we hope for and to live by principle in the meantime. There is no alternative, except surrender. And surrender abandons not only the future, it abandons the soul.

Subcommandante Marcos says, "History written by Power taught us that we had lost. . . . We did not believe what Power taught us. We skipped class when they taught conformity and idiocy. We failed modernity. We are united by the imagination, by creativity, by tomorrow. In the past we not only met defeat but also found a desire for justice and the dream of being better. We left skepticism hanging from the hook of big capital and discovered that we could believe, that it was worth believing, that we should believe—in ourselves. Health to you, and don't forget that flowers, like hope, are harvested."

And they grow in the dark. "I believe," adds Thoreau, "in the forest, and the meadow, and the night in which the corn grows."

JOURNEY TO THE
CENTER OF THE WORLD

The future is dark, but begin in the present, at the Pacific where it fronts my city, where western civilization comes to an end in a strip of sand and the realm of whales and sharks begins. Fish populations are plummeting in this and other oceans, but if you go down the coast a ways you'll come to where the sea otters hunted nearly into extinction have come back to the kelp beds; if you go either north or south, you'll come to the beaches where the elephant seals who were likewise nearly exterminated return every winter to fight, mate, and nurse their young. Take a third Pacific species, though—the brown pelican, which also nearly disappeared, then came back— and imagine one pelican's trajectory from Ocean Beach, the western edge of my city and our continent.

Imagine it soaring with the heavy prehistoric grace of a pterodactyl down Fulton Street, the long street that starts at the beach, parallels the north side of Golden Gate Park, and carries on after the park ends to run east through the old African-American neighborhood, past surviving gospel churches and extinct barbershops to the little

formal garden between the War Memorial Building and
the Opera House, then straight into City Hall, whose
great gilded dome straddles the street. Let that pelican
soar through the echoing central atrium where in 1961 students who protested the anticommunist purges were
washed down the marble stairs with fire hoses, let the bird
float out the other side, going on east, to United Nations
Plaza, where Fulton dead-ends into Market Street, the
city's main artery. This is the place where I stand in the
present to face past and future, the place where stories
come together, one of the countless centers of the world.

Just before the plaza is the Lick Monument, a colossal
Victorian confection of statuary, bas reliefs, and patriotic
inscriptions summing up California history as it looked
then. From the west, California as a fierce goddess con-
fronts you; at her feet stands the California grizzly, extinct
everywhere but in art and on the state flag. Dedicated on
Thanksgiving 1894, the monument survived the 1906
earthquake while all the buildings around it crumbled
and burned, and it was relocated when the new library
opened, almost a decade ago. During its relocation a few
Native Americans denounced one of its life-size sculptural groupings, the one that shows a Mexican *vaquero*
and *padre* looming ominously over a prone and apparently conquered Indian. They didn't succeed in getting
the statue removed, but they stirred up a furious public
conversation about California history, and they won an
addition, a bronze plaque below the sculptural group that

speaks of genocide and colonialism, a small rewriting of history, a small measure of change.

To the south of the monument is the new public library, built on the site of the Sandlot riots of 1877. The Sandlot was a space for free speech, but in 1877 the speech turned sordid, incitation to assault and arson against the Chinese population, a degeneration of the great antirailroad riots that spread across the country that summer when the United States came as close as it ever would to a full-fledged class war. But to the north, staring down the old Sandlot, is the superb new Asian Art Museum, a kind of redress or at least an address of the changing status of Asians in this part of America.

Across the street, in the plaza proper, is a bronze Simón Bolívar, the liberator of South America, on his rearing horse, sometimes with seagulls on his head, one day a year with a group of South American men leaving flowers as tribute. The plaza over whose western end Bolívar presides commemorates the 1945 founding of the United Nations a few blocks away in the War Memorial Building. Huge gold letters in the pavement spell out the preamble of the founding charter. "We the people of the United Nations determined to save the world from the scourge of war . . . to reaffirm faith in basic human rights, in the dignity and worth of the human person, in the equal rights of men and women, and of nations large and small," it begins. Two colonnades of stone pillar-streetlights are inscribed with the names of the member nations and the years they joined. There's a sort of secret dialogue among these monuments, a conversation about liberation—about imperfect solutions and unfinished revolutions—but still, liberation. And there's more literal sustenance here, too.

Every Wednesday and Sunday the plaza hosts a farmers' market, not one of the fancy boutique markets, but a big spread full of affordable food eagerly bought by the poor here in the supermarketless inner city, food grown and sold by Laotians, Latinos, old-time local whites—a small pragmatic United Nations of food production and urban-rural rendezvous. On those days the place is bustling, vibrant, full of the colors of roses, cherries, violet and lavender Chinese eggplant, honey, carrots, peppers, sunflowers, and many green things, full of people swinging bags of produce, haggling, hawking, greeting, walking over the words of the UN Charter.

The rest of the time it mostly belongs to the homeless, and so I go once a week to buy food from farmers and once a week to give it away to the destitute. Tuesdays I come here with a young monk from San Francisco Zen Center to feed the people who sit at Bolívar's feet, on the edges of the raised plantbeds and in the grimy surrounding streets. Sometimes the grander political causes are so abstract, so removed, it seems right instead to cook hot food, box it up in Chinese take-out cartons, and give out meals to fifty or sixty people. It's hard to say what difference we make, but we meet people who are hungry, people who bless us, and people who turn away because they're busy shooting up or crack has taken away their appetites or suffering has driven them mad. Few remember that there was no significant US homeless population before the 1980s, that Ronald Reagan's new society and economy created these swollen ranks of street people.

Even from City Hall you can see the huge letters of the artist Rigo '04's black, white, and silver mural across Market Street from U.N. Plaza, the letters that spell out TRUTH, and TRUTH is the far side of this constellation of histories. Rigo dedicated the mural to the Angola Three, the African-American political prisoners in Louisiana's Angola Prison. One of them, Robert King Wilkerson, was there for the dedication ceremony. A soft-spoken man, he spent twenty-nine years in solitary confinement for a murder he did not commit. He was framed for his political activism, then freed in 2001 thanks to the toil of volunteer lawyers — who are still working on the cases of the other two. A lot of the marches and demonstrations in San Francisco begin or end here, and so I've been here again and again for peace and justice as well as to get food and to give it away. This is what the world looks like to me, like U.N. Plaza, full of half-forgotten victories and new catastrophes, of farmers and junkies, of mountains of apples and of people trying to change the world and tell the truth. Someday all this may be ruins, but for now it is a place where history is still unfolding. Today is also the day of creation.

HOPE IN THE DOCK

I began writing about hope nearly two and a half years ago, as the Bush administration's war in Iraq was just beginning. In the years since, pretty much everything antiwar activists said before March 19, 2003—about the lack of Al Qaeda links and WMDs, about the brutality of wars and senselessness of this one—have become clear to everyone everywhere, except the administration. It has been a hideous war. And I am still hopeful, though at times over these years I seemed to be hope's defense lawyer in the criminal court of the media, alternative as well as mainstream.

Sometimes in these events I met splendid characters and heard amazing stories, and sometimes I was the headache medicine after a bout of drinking, the last bit of the program, as though I was going to undo the bad news that preceded me. Some interlocutors mistook hope for optimism or even for some insular state in which everything was already fine. Or they dismissed hope as though it were incompatible with the grievous outcome of one example or another they threw in my face: Bush is president, climate change exists. They considered any tragedy anywhere as a fatal blow against hope, as though it was a contract, a guarantee, not a belief in slender possibilities that sometimes, maybe, bear fruit.

I know Bush is president, and I know that the ravages of climate change have only begun. But it's the unknowns that are the grounds for hope, not the facts and likelihoods. In 2003, everyone knew who Bush was and that it was pretty likely he would still be president in 2005. And no one had heard of a woman in the uncelebrated town of Vacaville, California, named Cindy Sheehan, who did not yet know that her son Casey would die in Iraq on April 4, 2004, nor that she would become an outspoken political activist, the strongest voice against the war and against the president. As I write, Camp Casey has been outside the gates of Bush's ranch in Crawford, Texas, for more than two weeks, growing daily in numbers and significance, and Bush is a hostage to his own intransigence and unpopularity, with three weeks of his ranch vacation to go. Whether Cindy Sheehan and her community of families that lost loved ones to the war are really a tipping point for public opinion and the winding down of this unwinnable war remains to be seen. But her emergence out of nowhere and its absolute unforeseeability is part of my hope in the dark and sense of history's real workings.

The record shows that miracles are frequent but perfection never arrives. I don't believe in a perfect world, in the world without violence or war I recently heard a Jesuit activist describe. I believe that sometimes that vision of a better world is valuable and sometimes it's grounds for a grudge against the possible. I believe that violence and

war have been and are being and will be held back and
undermined some of the time, in some places, that peace
is often breaking out as the no news that is most of our
good news. In many places. Some of the time. Not in all.

Hope just means that change is all that is certain and
that what we do might matter, as Cindy Sheehan's public
protest against the war that took her son has come to
matter. It relies on uncertainty and ephemerality, on the
long track record of movements and individuals who
seemingly come out of nowhere and make a difference
somewhere, on the changes that would have been pre-
posterous as predictions but look inevitable in hindsight.
And this is grounds enough for never surrendering (as is
the principle of the thing: if the right would like me to
despair, hope is part of my defiance). Despair is in some
ways a form of certainty, mostly that the future extends
coherently from whatever is most grim in the present. And
political depression, like personal depression, seems to
bring the same kind of self-absorption, stuck in the here
and now in all the worst ways, as though this time will last
forever, as though this is the only place on earth.

For the Americans I was dealing with, it was as though
there were only two countries left on earth, Iraq and the
US, as though there had only been one election in 2004.
For me, South America was grounds for hope, not just
because the continent was afire with populist experiments
and potent civil societies—in Argentina, Brazil, Chile,

Ecuador, Venezuela, Uruguay—but because twenty years or so before, it had been a continent dominated by dictators, military rule, terror and repression. If that had changed so profoundly, perhaps anything could. And in 2004 elections, India's racist BJP party had been ousted, Uruguay had elected its first left-wing government in 170 years, Venezuela, forced into a plebescite by the US, had reelected the socialistic Hugo Chávez, and Spain had voted out its right-wing government.

Another test of hope I was often given was whether *everything* was going well; hope, in this version, was not compatible with a complex planet in which liberation movements and brutal wars flourish simultaneously. Asking for the impossible became an immunization against the effort hope requires. F. Scott Fitzgerald famously said, "The test of a first-rate intelligence is the ability to hold two opposed ideas in the mind at the same time, and still retain the ability to function." Fitzgerald's forgotten next sentence is, "One should, for example, be able to see that things are hopeless and yet be determined to make them otherwise." You wonder what made Václav Havel hopeful in 1985 or 1986, when Czechoslovakia was still a Soviet satellite and he was still a jailbird playwright.

Havel said then, long before his goals looked likely to many others, "The kind of hope I often think about (especially in situations that are particularly hopeless, such as prison) I understand above all as a state of mind, not a state of the world. Either we have hope within us or we don't; it is a dimension of the soul; it's not essentially dependent on some particular observation of the world or estimate of the situation. Hope is not prognostication. It is an orientation of the spirit, an orientation of the heart; it transcends the world that is immediately experienced, and is anchored somewhere beyond its horizons. Hope, in this deep and powerful sense, is not the same as joy that things are going well, or willingness to invest in enterprises that are obviously headed for early success, but, rather, an ability to work for something because it is good, not just because it stands a chance to succeed."

I still have a newspaper picture I clipped out during Czechoslovakia's 1989 Velvet Revolution, of some people in those heady days carrying a bust of Lenin, evidently on its way to the dump. It's adorned with the Czech phrase "*Nic Netra Vecne*"—nothing lasts forever. This is the last and least hope: that no nation or party will live forever, that time itself will repair some of what's wrong. But so much is at stake that hope must also be that our acts can matter.

Hope and action feed each other. There are people with good grounds for despair and a sense of helplessness: prisoners, the desperately poor, those overwhelmed by the labors of just surviving, those living under the threat of imminent violence. And there are less tangible reasons for inaction. When I think back to why I was apolitical into my mid-twenties I see that being politically engaged means having a sense of your own power—that what you do matters—and a sense of belonging to a group, a place, a cause, things that came to me only later and that do not come to everyone. Overcoming alienation and isolation or their causes is a political goal for the rest of us.

And for the rest of us, despair is more a kind of fatigue, a loss of faith, that can be overcome, or even at times a luxury if you look at the power of being political as a privilege not granted to everyone and at the cost of giving up as being far higher for those whose lives are more precarious or endangered. Though sometimes it's the most unlikely people who rise up and take power, the housewives and mothers who are supposed to be nobody, the prisoners who organize from inside, the people who have an intimate sense of what's at stake. You can frame it another way. The revolutionary Brazilian educator Paolo Freire wrote a sequel to his famous *Pedagogy of the Oppressed* called the *Pedagogy of Hope,* and in it he declares, "Without a minimum of hope, we cannot so much as start the struggle. But without the struggle, hope dissipates, loses its bearings, and turns into hopelessness. And hopelessness can turn into tragic despair. Hence the need for a kind of education in hope."

The despair that keeps coming up is a loss of belief that the struggle is worthwhile. That loss comes from many quarters, from exhaustion, from a sadness born out of empathy, but also from expectations and analyses that are themselves problems. "Resistance is the secret of joy" said a banner carried by Reclaim the Streets in the late 1990s, quoting Alice Walker. Resistance is first of all a matter of principle and a way to live, to make yourself one small republic of unconquered spirit. You hope for results, but you don't depend on them. And if you study the historical record, there have been results, as suprising as Czechoslovakia's 1989 Velvet Revolution, and there will be more. As Freire points out, struggle generates hope as it goes along. Waiting until everything looks feasible is too long to wait.

I quoted Freire to a group of blue-collar, mostly non-white night-school students as part of a talk on hope that was hard to give, because the students seemed far better qualified than I to weigh the subject. But they spoke up about emigration, racism, activism, books, joy, and their daily lives in Washington State, and the very subject of hope seemed to make them passionate. A slender, elegant woman of about my age spoke up in a small clear voice about Freire. "I think that is right," she said, "because if I did not hope, I would not have struggled. And if I had not struggled, I would not have survived the Khmer Rouge."

My argument for hope has three threads. One makes the case that our history of victories and the degree of transformation of our societies for the better is far more profound than we ordinarily remember and standard histories record. One suggests that change takes place in more protracted, circuitous, surprising ways than is often acknowledged, so that disappointment is often based on the wrong expectations or calculations. And one challenges the case for despair, the Eeyore chorus out there. Following are two new chapters, or afterwords, for this book I will never truly finish. One expands on the investigation of how victory can be measured—and mismeasured or dismissed. The other suggests that those looking at how dismal everything is are sometimes overlooking the places that matter most.

THE GREAT GRAY WHALE, OR, THIS STORY HAS NO MORAL

While we were looking at humpback whales a few months ago, my companion asked me if I ever thought about how *Moby-Dick*'s narrator, Ishmael, survived—by floating away from the destroyed ship *Pequod* in his friend Queequeg's coffin. Whales themselves survived into the twenty-first century in part because of petroleum, the black stuff seeping out of the Pennsylvania earth that made the Rockefellers rich and whale oil unnecessary for lighting lamps (and because of the first international whaling treaty in 1949). Of course, petroleum went on to create the climate change that threatens the habitat for whales and devastates their realm in other ways. There is no easy moral to this, any more than there is to Ishmael floating away safely because his friend had terrible premonitions of death. And that's part of the richness of Herman Melville's telling.

The world is full of tales in which morals are hard to extract from facts. There is the delightful fact that Viagra has been good for endangered species now less at risk of being ground up for Asian aphrodisiacs, surely the greatest inadvertent contribution of big pharmaceuticals in our time. Casinos have provided many Native American tribes with revenue and clout, though gambling is another kind of social problem and outside groups are the principal profiteers from some of the casinos. McDonald's has (under intense pressure from animal rights activists) led the way in reforming how meat animals are raised and slaughtered. Many military sites have become de facto wildlife refuges, saving huge swaths of land from civilian development (even if bombing endangered species is part of the drill). Even the Korean DMZ is full of endangered birds and plants.

Then there are those interesting moments when otherwise appalling politicians do something decent for whatever reason or when the principled and the sinister are weirdly mixed—like anti-abortion, pro-death-penalty Arizona Senator John McCain's passion for addressing climate change or the recently deceased Pope John Paul II's condemnation of neoliberalism. To say nothing of our one great environmental president, Richard Nixon (and it wasn't out of purity of heart that Nixon got us the Environmental Protection Agency, the Endangered Species Act, and the Clean Air and Water Acts, but purity of water and air matter more).

Sometimes, though, I think my compatriots are looking for the real world to provide stories as simple as Sunday school and sports, not as complex as *Moby-Dick*. I would like those victories too. I would have liked it a lot if, after returning from the G8 summit in Gleneagles, Scotland, in July 2005, George W. Bush had—in a live global telecast, like the Oscars—fallen to his knees, apologized profusely to everyone for everything, condemned capitalism, violence, and himself, promised to dismantle the World Bank and the International Monetary Fund, and to stop the war in Iraq immediately, and to dedicate some of the billions thus saved to African poverty. And that's just for starters. But let's look instead at what we got from the G8, the annual meeting of the world's seven fattest economies, plus Russia.

Bush, as ever, refused to deal with climate change and was dragged along only grudgingly on aid and debt-relief measures for Africa. Even so, in the lead-up to the summit, eighteen of the world's poorest nations, including Bolivia, Ethiopia, Ghana, Nicaragua, Rwanda, and Uganda, received a 100 percent cancellation of foreign debt—a $40 billion write-off from the International Monetary Fund, the World Bank, and the African Development Bank.

Nine more countries will receive debt cancellation in the next eighteen months. Of course, there were strings attached—preexisting policies obliging those nations to play by some of the rules that made them destitute to begin with.

A lot of radicals excoriated the whole business of the G8 taking up debt relief and African poverty. John Pilger wrote in the *New Statesman:* "It is a fraud—actually a setback to reducing poverty in Africa. Entirely conditional on vicious, discredited economic programmes imposed by the World Bank and the IMF, the 'package' will ensure that the 'chosen' countries slip deeper into poverty. Is it any surprise that this is backed by Blair and his treasurer, Gordon Brown, and George Bush; even the White House calls it a 'milestone'?"

Others disagreed. Foreign Policy in Focus analyst Mark Engler wrote: "Those progressives who have attacked the debt deal emphasize that, even in announcing the cancellation, G8 finance ministers explicitly reaffirm a neoliberal economic paradigm. Under the new G8 agreement, eighteen countries do receive full debt cancellation from the IMF and World Bank, and nine other countries may be granted similar relief at a later date. . . . This breakthrough represents a significant victory. . . . In one example, some 2.2 million people in Uganda gained access to water as a result of a post-1997 debt cancellation."

The debate seems to be over whether this is capitulation or incremental victory. The majority of victories are muddled, compromised, incomplete, and uncredited. It is no surprise that Blair and Bush failed to excoriate themselves or the system that creates poverty. Of course, they avoided systemic analysis while claiming to have always been on the side of the angels. Radicals often want a victory that is sudden, dramatic, and full of moral illumination, that belongs clearly to them and to them alone, the kind where the other side loudly repents and credits you with dramatically reversing their course, or better yet simply surrenders and leaves the arena. This is not even victory, but vindication, since the focus shifts from alleviating suffering to acknowledging its cause and your virtue.

I remember when some portion of California's Headwaters Forest was saved after a long struggle on the part of Earth First! and other environmental radicals. That there was outrage over the inadequate protection was one thing; that so many were instead focused on the fact that junk bond king Charles Hurwitz, owner of Pacific Lumber, had profited handsomely from selling the land was about a real slip in focus from saving trees to thwarting opponents. It would have been nice to see Hurwitz penniless and in jail, and there were good reasons why he should be both—but the forest was more important and saving it had been the point all along. It wasn't about Puritan morality, in which the punishment of sinners is the point, but about life, in which survival of the rest matters more.

It's often true that what we need is systemic change and nothing less, but humanitarianism often means accepting lesser steps along the way, and sometimes those steps lead toward something more revolutionary. A friend pointed out to me that when your client is facing the death penalty, you might like to abolish capital punishment and reform the system, but your courtroom victory will consist first of all in keeping him off death row.

A more complicated parable I heard fifteen years ago was made memorable by the teller, just out of jail for destroying nuclear missile guidance systems. She described a group of washerwomen on a riverbank who see a baby floating along, rescue it, and then find themselves plunging into the river regularly to grab babies. Finally one washerwoman walks away from the scene. Her comrades ask her if she doesn't care about babies. She replies, "I'm going to go upstream to find the guy who's throwing them in." She is the revolutionary ideologue who will take on the system, but in the meantime there's something to be said for pulling out the babies who will drown before— in the case of debt relief—the end of neoliberalism. Both are needed and they can be symbiotic rather than competing positions. There are a lot of babies at stake.

And getting the guy who's throwing them in might not be the same thing as establishing the principle that babies should never become flotsam. Or it might. As antiglobalization scholar Antonia Juhasz wrote me, "If corporate globalization worked, these countries would not only be out of debt, they'd be in the black. By conceding the need for debt cancellation, they [the rich countries] have in fact ceded the failure of the model. Therefore, a new door has opened to us to demonstrate that the other elements of the model are failures as well and therefore must be eliminated—next in line are the Structural Adjustment Programs and the conditionalities." Which is to say that accepting the limited victory of the summer of 2005 concedes nothing.

When politicians are involved, Gandhi's famous dictum could be revised to read: "First they ignore you, then they laugh at you, then they fight you, then they co-opt your issue and pretend it was always theirs, and then if you don't get all muddled, you still might win." It won't look like victory. It won't satisfy the way victory is supposed to satisfy. It will come in dribbles rather than in a glorious burst; it will arrive in the hands of those you loathe; it will appear in some unanticipated form hard to recognize. Changes come sneakily, like the thieves they are, stealing the familiar world. By the time you win, your victory no longer belongs to you; it belongs first to the annoying former adversaries who have taken it up and now espouse it as though it had always been their own, and then it belongs to history.

Maybe we have team sports so that every once in a blue moon something will look like victory. And every once in a while the real world has its watersheds—Mandela's inauguration, say—rather than just its trickles. In Mexico, the seventy-year dictatorship of the PRI ended not with a Mandela but with ex–Coca-Cola executive Vicente Fox assuming the presidency—though this may yet open the way for left-wing Mexico City Mayor Lopez Obrador to become that country's president next year in what would be, twenty years on from the first loosening of the PRI's stranglehold, a real victory after murky, incremental changes that may make it possible.

But victories are slippery things. For radicals in the US, nothing has been more definitively successful than the shutdown of the WTO in Seattle in 1999. A clear-cut victory, but corporate globalization has turned out to be, like the hydra of Greek mythology, hard to slay. When you cut off the hydra's head, more heads grew in its place, and when the WTO was stymied, regional and bilateral trade agreements in the mode of NAFTA succeeded it. So the victory in Seattle was tremendous, and the battle is far from over.

The real debate is over perception: radicals fear that the acceptance of limited changes undermines the profound change they seek, and the less radical are indeed often willing to accept palliative measures instead. But intermediary incremental change undermines that larger goal only if it is perceived as final and adequate. Perhaps what is needed from both is an ability to hail achievements without regarding them as occasions to quit and to recognize that change will shuffle more often than leap. Of course, when it comes to who demands what and who decides what comes next, it's more complicated. And limited changes can be how politicians, in their traditional "we're only killing half as many as before" way, disarm popular outcry rather than truly address what's at stake.

I was in England and Scotland a month before the G8 talks. Prime Minister Tony Blair had taken up climate change and African relief in what appeared to be a blatant bait-and-switch on the war in Iraq he had gotten his country into, and it had worked—that war was a minor news story by comparison and a relatively minor issue in the G8 protests. (This was, of course, before the London bombings that July brought the question of Iraq back onto the front pages.)

A searching national conversation on the real causes of African poverty was going on—with various conclusions. To explain that disaster spread over most of a continent, some pointed to a half-millennium of European colonization and genocide and its political and psychological aftermath; some to widespread support for corrupt and undemocratic regimes that milk their countries dry; others to the role pillaging multinational corporations play in draining Africa of its natural wealth. All are causes, of course, as are the policies of the IMF and the World Bank. But the question that fascinated me was: What had caused African poverty to move to the center of British national consciousness and G8 negotiations?

Seven years earlier, I had been at the demonstrations against the 1998 G8 Summit in Birmingham, England. This was seventeen months before the epochal shutdown of the World Trade Organization in Seattle fittingly exiled the unloved leaders of the more or less free world to meeting in self-created super-militarized zones. (Security for this summit in rural Scotland cost hundreds of millions of pounds. One Scottish local commented that they should have met on an aircraft carrier in the middle of the ocean—in the cheaper and more honest armed isolation that would best represent their relationship to the public.)

In '98, I had gone to Birmingham to hang out with Reclaim the Streets (RTS), the raucous, wildly creative British movement that shifted the tone and tactics of direct action in many parts of the world and demonstrated early the power of the Internet for creating simultaneous demonstrations in many countries. At the same moment, Jubilee 2000 (now Jubilee Research) formed a vast human chain around the G8 and much of central Birmingham. RTS condemned the G8's very existence; Jubilee 2000 asked it for something specific. At the time, the jubilee group made little impression on me, and their "Cancel the Debt" message seemed hopeful but remote. It is impressive to measure the migration of the idea of debt cancellation (and so, the role of the wealthiest nations in creating poverty) as it traveled from outside the walls of Birmingham into Gleneagles as the unavoidable topic.

No less impressive is the way the early champions of debt relief took up such a complex, unglamorous idea and stuck with it for so long—long enough to matter, long enough to change the world.

For debt relief exemplifies the often murky issues of much contemporary activism. Everyone agrees that children shouldn't be murdered, but it's hard to show how arcane and intricate international financial rules can become the swords upon which small bodies are impaled. Zambia announced that cancellation of its debt will immediately translate into anti-retrovirals for some of its 100,000 AIDS sufferers (which exemplifies, as well, how debt translates into death; think of all those who did not get medication because of internationally created debt and poverty).

Win or lose, the question of what was achieved begs a larger question: Is it useful to hail less-than-perfect, less-than-complete achievements? There is a real danger of complacency if the assessment is simplified into "we won," since winning in this culture is usually followed by going home, as if life on earth was a game that ended when your team had the higher score. But there is also danger in never acknowledging the victories that do occur on this strange planet. For then you leave bystanders, newcomers, sometimes even old-timers with the impression that we never win, that nothing we do works, that we have no power.

Toughness, critique, dissatisfaction always have an important place in reminding people that the game isn't up and suffering continues; so does recognizing that real change is possible and that activists have real power. It's not black or white, not cause for resting on laurels or for despair, just for continuing on with the endless project of a better world. Moby Dick was white; the humpback whales I saw spouting and leaping in the Pacific were nearly black; but truth and history are larger, and grayer.

A History of Shadows

Imagine the world as a theater. The acts of the powerful and the official occupy center stage. The traditional versions of history, the conventional sources of news encourage us to fix our gaze on that stage. The limelights there are so bright they blind you to the shadowy spaces around you, make it hard to meet the gaze of the other people in the seats, to see the way out of the audience, into the aisles, backstage, outside, in the dark, where other powers are at work. A lot of the fate of the world is decided onstage, in the limelight, and the actors there will tell you that no other place matters.

What is onstage is a tragedy, the tragedy of the inequitable distribution of power and of the too-common silence of those who settle for being audience while paying the price of the drama. Traditionally, the audience is supposed to choose the actors, and the actors are quite literally supposed to speak for us. This is the idea behind representative democracy. In practice, various reasons keep many from participating in the choice, other forces—like money—subvert that choice, and onstage too many of the actors find other reasons— lobbyists, self-interest, conformity—to fail to represent their constituents.

The people who rebuke me about the terrible state of the world and the shaky grounds for hope always point to the limelight, to the figures on center stage, to Bush, to Blair, to armies and corporations, to the status quo, as though this week's version of power was immortal and eternal, as though one could not look back to a different world not long ago that augurs a different world to come—better or worse, but not the same. They speak as though we should wait for improvement to be handed to us, not as though we might seize it. Perhaps their despair is in some ways simply that they are audience rather than actors.

The grounds for hope are in the shadows, in the people who are inventing the world while no one looks, who themselves don't know yet whether they will have any effect, in the people you have not yet heard of who will be the next Cesar Chavez, the next Noam Chomsky, the next Cindy Sheehan, or become something you cannot yet imagine. In this epic struggle between light and dark, it's the dark side—that of the anonymous, the unseen, the officially powerless, the visionaries and subversives in the shadows—that we must hope for. For those onstage, we can just hope the curtain comes down soon and the next act is better, that it comes more directly from the populist shadows.

If you pointed to Spain's tyrant Francisco Franco during his reign from 1939 to 1975, you would point to the worst that had already happened; hope's grounds were instead in the people who had not stopped dreaming of liberty and justice and who got democracy—through the unlikely avenue of King Juan Carlos's reformist urges— soon after Franco's death. Even the most hopeful could not have foreseen that in 2004, the Spanish would vote in a Socialist government that immediately withdrew from the war in Iraq and in 2005 made same-sex marriage the law of the land. Franco's tomb, built by the forced labor of Civil War prisoners, has been transformed by this new government into a monument to democracy.

On center stage nowadays is the most environmentally destructive administration in US history. But swarming out of the edges are activists and organizations with creative tactics. The US Conference of Mayors passed a resolution supporting the Kyoto Protocol, and Seattle led the way for cities across the country to go green; the states are setting much higher emissions standards for cars and other states setting power plant emissions standards far more stringent than the administrations; Rainforest Action Network succeeded in getting major corporations from Citicorp to Boise Cascade to back off from participating in destruction of pristine forests.

Turn your head. Learn to see in the dark. Pay attention to the inventive arenas that exert political power outside that stage or change the contents of the drama onstage. From the places that you have been instructed to ignore or rendered unable to see come the stories that change the world, and it is here that culture has the power to shape politics and ordinary people have the power to change the world. Often it appears as theater, and you can see the baffled, upset faces of the actors onstage when the streets become a stage or the unofficial appear among them to disrupt the planned program. George Bush's alarm when Cindy Sheehan made him at last genuinely accountable for the real impacts of his war— when she rather than he set the agenda—is a fine example.

A literature of hope is gathering these days. In 1785, no one in Britain was thinking about slavery, except slaves, ex-slaves, and a few Quakers and soft-hearted evangelicals. In his 2005 book *Bury the Chains*, Adam Hochschild tells the story of how the dozen or so original activists gathered at a London printer's shop. From that point onward this handful of hopefuls created a movement that in half a century abolished slavery in the British Empire and helped spark the abolition movement that ended slavery in the United States a quarter-century or so later. Part of the story is about the imagination and determination of a few key figures.

But part of it is about a change of heart whereby enough people came to believe that slavery was an intolerable cruelty to bring its day to an end, despite the profitability of the institution to the powerful who defended it. It was arguments, sermons, editorials, pamphlets, conversations that changed the mind of the public: stories, for the decisions were mostly made in London (encouraged by witnesses and slave revolts abroad). The atrocities were mostly out of sight of the audience. It required imagination, empathy, and information to make abolition a cause and then a victory. In those five decades antislavery sentiments went from being radical to being the status quo, as slavery went from being invisible to a principal political and moral issue.

Stories move a little faster in our own time. It has taken less than forty years for homosexuality to go from being classified as a crime and a mental disorder to being widely accepted as part of the variety of ordinary, everyday life. There is a backlash, but backlashes for all their viciousness cannot turn back the clock or put the genie back in his lamp. Like views of slavery, the change has come so incrementally it can only be measured in court decisions and opinion polls, but it did not come as naturally as a

change in the weather. It was *made* by activists, but also by
artists, writers, comedians, and filmmakers who asserted
other versions of sexuality, other kinds of family, by all
those parade organizers and marchers, by millions of ordinary individuals living openly as gay or lesbian to their
families and communities, by people leaving behind their
fears and animosities. Along similar lines, shifts in thought
that led to activism and then shifts in law have radically
revised the lives and rights of the disabled.

You may be told that legal decisions lead the changes,
that judges and lawmakers lead the culture in those the-
aters called courtrooms, but they only ratify change. They
are almost never where change begins, only where it ends
up, for most changes travel from the edges to the center.
How did these stories and beliefs migrate from the margins? The routes are seldom discussed or even explored,
in part because so much attention is focused on that central stage. The edges are literally marginal—the margins
—but they are also portrayed as dangerous and unsavory.
One of the great shocks of recent years came to me in a
police station in Scotland, where in the course of
reporting a lost wallet I found myself contemplating a
poster of wanted criminals: not rapists and murderers but
kids with peculiar hairstyles and piercings who had been
active in demonstrations such as the Carnival Against
Capital and other frolics in which business as usual had
been disrupted but no one had been harmed. So these

were the criminals who most threatened the state? Then
the state was fragile and we were powerful.

In the US, the Bush administration, the mainstream
media, and many mayors and chiefs of police have portrayed as terrorists—as bomb planters, acid-throwers,
police assailants—activists employing the First Amendment's guarantee of the right to speak and assemble
and the nonviolent tactics of Gandhi and King. Other
governments—notably Britain's with those wanted posters
and the 1994 Criminal Justice Act—have done the same.
They willfully, if not consciously, mistake what kind of
danger these street activists pose, as they have before,
when civil rights advocates, suffragists, and abolitionists
were being persecuted. To admit that these people pose a
threat to the status quo is to admit first that there is a status
quo, secondly that it may be an unjust and unjustifiable
thing, and thirdly that it can indeed be changed by passionate people and nonviolent means. To admit this is to
admit the limits of their power and its legitimacy. Better to
marginalize activists—to portray them as rabble on the
fringe who are dangerous the way violent criminals are
dangerous. Thus is both the power and the legitimacy of
the margins denied. Denied by those in the limelight, but
you don't have to believe them.

I used to. Thinking about how things that once seemed
impossibly distant came to pass, I am embarrassed to
remember how dismissive of the margins I once was, fifteen

or so years ago, when I secretly scoffed at the shanty-towns built on college campuses as part of the anti-apartheid movement. That people were protesting something so remote and entrenched seemed futile. But then the divestment of college funds from corporations doing business with South Africa became part of the sanctions movement, and the sanctions movement prodded along the end of apartheid. What lies ahead seems unlikely; when it becomes the past, it seems inevitable. In 1900, the idea that women should have the vote was revolutionary; now, the idea that we should not have it would seem cracked. But no one went back to apologize to the suffragists who chained themselves to the gates of power, smashed all the windows on Bond Street, spent long months in jail, suffered forced feed-ings and demonization in the press.

I thought about this again when I was reading a superb story on the Pennsylvania townships seeking to abolish corporate personhood—the legal status that gives corpo-rations a dangerous and undemocratic range of rights in the US. It seemed like one of those ideas that might be migrating toward the center, but in twenty years if *Time* magazine is questioning the shift from democracy to a sort of monarchy of corporations or the *New York Times* is reporting the overturning of the legal principles on which corporate hegemony rests, they won't thank a bunch of radical professors or scruffy anticapitalist street activists who were being tear-gassed for arguing the point prematurely. There will never be a moment when someone in the Senate or on national TV news will say, "Those freaks in the underbrush saw the future when we on high were blind." Instead, the perils of corporate personhood will become common sense, become what everyone always knew. Which is to say, stories migrate secretly. The assumption that whatever we now believe is just common sense, or what we always knew, is a way to save face. It's also a way to forget the power of a story and of a storyteller, the power in the margins, and the potential for change.

Forty-three years ago, the Colorado River was dammed at Glen Canyon and the exquisitely labyrinthine sandstone landscape of canyons, curtain walls, arches, caves, sacred sites, petroglyphs, and ruins were buried in a man-made lake that backed up more than a hundred miles from the dam. Downstream, much was ravaged as well, including survival odds for the rough river's unique fish. The environmentalists who had fought it thought that they were saying goodbye to that fabulous landscape and to the ecosystem that depended upon the river currents forever.

Thirty years ago, Edward Abbey wrote a novel, *The Monkey Wrench Gang*, in which his heroes plot to blow up Glen Canyon Dam, the huge desert dam strangling the Colorado River upstream from the Grand Canyon. Getting rid of the dam was an outrageous idea then, though the novel helped spark the birth of the radical environmental organization Earth First! In 1981, the group announced its existence by running a 300-foot sheet of plastic bearing the image of a mighty crack down the dam, which never seemed quite so eternal and immutable again. And the term "monkey wrench" entered the American vocabulary as a term for sabotage or other physical interventions for political purposes.

Recently, the idea of taking down the dam or permanently opening its spillways has come to seem more and more reasonable and even possible (the fact that long-term drought has dropped the reservoir water level to 37 percent capacity doesn't hurt either). The dam was designed to store surplus water, but the thirsty agricultural and urban river drinkers may never again leave a surplus to store, and water flow is likely to decrease in this warming era. The dam that even its enemies thought was forever has not even made it to the half-century mark. The hunk of concrete is intact, but its reasons have trickled away. More than 145 smaller US dams have already been dismantled, and dams have come down across Europe; the new era has already begun to slip in quietly.

One of the stories my friend Chip Ward follows in his book *Hope's Horizon* is about how the idea of dismantling Glen Canyon Dam is gaining support. If it happens, it will come to look like it always was a good idea, and the first people to espouse it will be forgotten, since they were kooks, extremists, and impractical dreamers. No one in the center will remember when they supported what now looks like bad science and bad engineering, just as few remember when they supported segregation or bans on mixed-race marriages. Their amnesia is necessary to their sense of legitimacy in a society they would rather not acknowledge is in constant change.

Chip wrote me the other day, "As an activist, I have observed that if a story is controversial in nature and threatens the powerful I may have to 'inoculate' it first by giving it to a young journalist who has more tolerance for risk from some alternative weekly that is also more edgy. The next step up the food chain may be a public radio station. After the story appears and the homework is done, if nobody is sued, then I can get a reporter from an established newspaper to write about it or get a television reporter on it. This is partly because newspaper reporters have to convince editors who are a skittish bunch who answer to suits who have their eyes on advertisers and the corporate guys over them who play golf with the people who may be criticized in the story." This certainly does seem like a food chain, though a food chain in reverse, perhaps, since the television networks are, in Chip's view, eating the alternative media's excretions.

Chip, incidentally, moved to Utah and eventually became one of that state's most potent environmental activists because his brother-in-law read another Ed Abbey book, *Desert Solitaire*, moved there himself, and sent back reports of how glorious the red-rock canyons were. And so Abbey, who was a reluctant activist with sometimes problematic politics, played a huge role in prompting some of the fiercest activists of our time.

And the group whose creation Abbey helped to inspire spawned a British branch of Earth First! that metamorphosed into the powerful antiroads movement of the mid-1990s, perhaps the most successful direct-action campaign in recent British history. More than five hundred road-building schemes were canceled. And from the anti-roads movement came Reclaim the Streets, which sparked many of the creative tactics and attitudes that gave the Northern Hemisphere something to contribute to the movement against corporate globalization at the end of the 1990s and changed the face of activism. Abbey's books weren't the only seeds for these transformations, and it's only because they aren't so deep in the shadows that their influence can be traced; beyond them are countless other sources for change.

Stories move from the shadows to the limelight. And though the stage too often presents the drama of our powerlessness, the shadows offer the secret of our power. This book is a history of the shadows and of the darkness in which hope lies.

ACKNOWLEDGMENTS

For twenty years my brother David has kept me connected to the activism in the streets he organizes, given me his view of what's going on, and worked with me on his projects and mine. He has been a radicalizing influence so huge that I cannot imagine what my writing would be without him, and so devotion, friendship, and gratitude to him and to the rest of the crew that helped me pull this book together. To my editor, Tom Engelhardt, who was there with encouragement and insight from the beginning; to John Jordan, for transcontinental inspiration, encouragement, and conversation; to Jake Kosek for a brilliant close reading of and commentary on the first draft. Thanks as well to these people who took time to talk to me about ideas in the book: Pame Kingfisher, Roxanne Dunbar-Ortiz, Carl Anthony, Jonathan Schell, Eddie Yuen, Chip Ward, Jaime Cortez, Mark Rudd, Laurie Lane-Zucker. And to my wartime affinity group, BADASS, the Bay Area Direct Action Secret Society, Tina, Heather, Dan, Julian, Paul, Leigh, Julia, Evan; my Nevada posse, particularly Kaitlin, Bob, Marla, and Jo Anne; and to Code Orange affinity group in Miami in November.

NOTES

1

1 Virginia Woolf wrote, "The future is dark . . .": *The Diary of Virginia Woolf* (Harcourt, New York, 1981). Vol. 1

5 Ernst Bloch wrote, "The work of this emotion": in *The Principle of Hope*, Vol. 1, translated by Neville Plaice, Stephen Plaice, and Paul Knight (Cambridge, MA: The MIT Press, 1986), 3.

2

8 Alphonso Lingis says, "Hope is hope against the evidence": in Mary Zournazi, editor and interviewer, *Hope: New Philosophies for Change* (New York: Routledge, 2003), 23–24.

10 Mike Van Winkle, "You can make an easy kind of a link": *Oakland Tribune*, May 17, 2003.

11 Tom Engelhardt points out that the girl in the Vietnam photograph, like Ali Abbas, was one of the lucky ones: visibility led to public outrage and compassion, which led to medical treatment abroad for both of them.

3

13 Ernst Bloch, *Principle of Hope*, 5.

19 Michael Taussig, in Mary Zournazi, *Hope: New Philosophies for Change*, 61.

4

24 Gary Younge writes, "The anti-war movement got the German chancellor": *Guardian* (London) online, October 6, 2003.

5

31 Václav Havel, "It was not a bolt out of the blue": *Living in Truth: Twenty-Two Essays Published on the Occasion of the Award of the Erasmus Prize to Václav Havel*, edited by Jan Vladislav (London: Faber and Faber, 1987), 66.

6

34 Elizabeth Martinez notes, "Rooted in the democratic, community-based culture" in David Solnit, ed., *Globalize Liberation* (San Francisco: City Lights, 2004), from manuscript.

36 Manuel Callahan quote in "A Few Theses on Zapatismo," *Globalize Liberation*, from manuscript.

38 George Orwell wrote, "full of revolutionary sentiments": *Homage to Catalonia* (New York: Harcourt Brace and Company, 1980), 42.

39 Fourth Declaration of the Lacandon Jungle, "A new lie is being sold to us as history": quoted in Gustavo Esteva and Madhu Suri Prakash, *Grassroots Postmodernism: Remaking the Soil of Cultures* (New York: Zed Books, 1998), 43.

7

44 Charles Derber writes, "The excitement of Seattle was the subliminal sense": *People Before Profit: The New Globalization in an Age of Terror, Big Money, and Economic Crisis* (New York: St. Martin's Press, 2002), 203.

45 Jose Bové, "I had the feeling that a new period": Jose Bové and Francois Dufour, *The World Is Not for Sale: Farmers Against Junk Food*, interviewed by Gilles Luneau, translated by Anna de Casparis (London and New York: Verso, 2001), 161.

45 Iain Boal wrote, "The longing for a better world": "Up from the Bottom," in Elaine Katzenberg, ed., *First World, Ha Ha Ha!* (San Francisco: City Lights Books, 1995), 173.

47 Eddie Yuen wrote, "One of the most influential strands": in Eddie Yuen, George Katsiaficas, Daniel Burton Rose, eds., *The Battle of Seattle: The New Challenge to Capitalist Globalization* (New York: Soft Skull Press, 2001), 11.

9

55 Robert Muller exclaimed, "I'm so honored to be alive": in the web-

site of westbynorthwest.org, Lynne Twist, "Waging Peace: A Story about Robert Muller," March 14, 2003.

10

58 Gandhi said, "First they ignore you": in Notes from Nowhere Collective, eds., *We Are Everywhere: The Irresistible Rise of Global Anticapitalism* (London and New York: Verso, 2003), 500.

11

65 Sharon Salzberg consigned the project to the "minor-good-deed category": in *Faith: Trusting Your Own Deepest Experience* (New York: Riverhead Books, 2002), 139–140.

67 Jorge Luis Borges, "You live and will die in this prison": in "Inferno, I, 32," *Labyrinths* (Harmondsworth, England: Penguin Books, 1970), 273.

70 Borges, "Dante, in wonderment," ibid., 275.

71 Walter Benjamin wrote, "Every line we succeed in publishing today": January 11, 1940, quoted in Lloyd Spencer, online extracts from *Benjamin for Beginners*.

12

73 Benjamin writes, "This is how one pictures the angel": "Theses on the Philosophy of History," in *Illuminations: Essays and Reflections* (New York: Schocken Books, 1969), 257.

74 Citizen Alert's biggest victory was achieved in coalition, of course, with various other regional and antinuclear groups.

75 Who talks about the global elimination of smallpox between 1967 and 1977? The 2003 *Worldwatch Report* does, and that's where I was reminded of it.

13

78 Chip Ward in *Hope's Horizon* (Island Press, 2004), from manuscript.

79 Richard White, "The Natures of Nature Writing," *Raritan*, Winter 2002, 161.

180

REBECCA SOLNIT

14

83 Eduardo Galeano, "Utopia is on the horizon": *We Are Everywhere*, 499.

85 Milan Kundera, *The Book of Laughter and Forgetting* (Harmondsworth, England: Penguin Books, 1981), from the interview by Philip Roth with the author, 233.

86 John Keats called the world "this vale of soul-making": Philip Levine, "On First Looking into John Keats's Letters," *Doubletake*, Spring 1996, 139.

86 Gopal Dayaneni said, "I have a soul": "War on Iraq: The Home Front," *San Francisco Chronicle*, March 25, 2003.

87 Walter Benjamin wrote, "The class struggle . . . is a fight for the crude and material things": "Theses on the Philosophy of History," in *Illuminations*, 254.

88 Hakim Bey contrasted these moments of uprising with revolutions proper, which "lead to the expected curve," in the online version of T.A.Z.

15

91 June Jordan writes, "We should take care": "Notes Toward a Black Balancing of Love and Hatred," in *Some of Us Did Not Die*, 285.

98 Lynne Sherrod recalls, "The environmentalists and the ranchers were squared off": Phil Huffman, interview with Lynne Sherrod, *Orion Afield*, Summer 2000, 19.

99 William DeBuys writes, "a departure from business as usual": "Looking for the 'Radical Center' " in *Forging a West that Works: An Invitation to the Radical Center* (Santa Fe: The Quivera Coalition, 2003), 51.

99 Baldemar Velasquez says, "Number one, I don't consider anybody opposition": interview with the author, September 2003.

16

103 Cornel West defined jazz "not so much as a term for a musical art form": *Race Matters* (Boston: Beacon Books, 1993), 150.

104 Charles Derber calls this the "third wave": *People Before Profit*, 205.

104 Naomi Klein wrote of the anti-globalization activists a few years ago, "When critics say the protesters lack vision": in "The Vision Thing," *The Battle of Seattle*, 314.

105 Naomi Klein, "non-hierarchical decisionmaking": "The Unknown Icon," Tom Hayden, ed. *The Zapatista Reader* (New York: Thunder's Mouth Press/Nation Books, 2002), 121.

105 John Jordan writes, "Our movements are trying to create": e-mail to the author, August 2003.

107 Alphonso Lingis says, "We really have to free the notion of liberation": in Mary Zournazi, *Hope: New Philosophies for Change*, 38.

108 Or as my brother David writes, "The notion of capturing positions of power": introduction to *Globalize Liberation*, from manuscript.

108 Giaconda Belli writes, "Two days that felt as if a magical": *The Country Under My Skin: A Memoir of Love and War* (New York: Alfred A. Knopf, 2003), 291.

108 Raoul Vaneigem writes, "Revolutionary moments are carnivals": quoted in *Do or Die* (Earth First! Britain's newsletter), issue 6, 1997, 4.

17

109 Danny Postel, "Gray's Anatomy" (review), *The Nation*, Dec. 22, 2003, p. 44.

111 Jim Dodge, "Living by Life: Some Bioregional Theory and Practice," in Lorraine Anderson, Scott Slovic, John P. O'Grady, eds., *Literature and the Environment: A Reader on Nature and Culture* (New York: Longman, 1999), 233.

112 Eddie Yuen writes of "commitment to direct democracy": *The Battle of Seattle*, ibid.

114 Arundhati Roy writes of "the dismantling of the Big": quoted in Paul Hawken, "The End of Sustainability," *Bioneers Letter*, Spring 2003, 11.

18

119 George Monbiot wrote, "At Cancún the weak nations stood up to the most powerful": "A Threat to the Rich," *Guardian* online, September 15, 2003.

120 As Peter Rosset of Food First tells it, "Everyone feared the worst sort of confrontation": online report, Food First website, September 2003.

121 Rosset says, "our collective ability to do the unexpected": ibid.

122 Schell quotes John Adams saying that the American Revolution "was in the minds of the people": *The Unconquerable World: Power, Nonviolence, and the Will of the People* (New York: Metropolitan Books, 2003), 160.

122 "In the new world of politically committed and active people": ibid.

123 "Individual hearts and minds change": ibid.

19

127 Roxanne Dunbar-Ortiz, conversation with the author, October 2003.

131 John Amagoalik remembers in "Wasteland of Nobodies," in Jens Dall, Jack Hicks, and Peter Jull, eds., *Nunavut: Inuit Regain Control of Their Lands and Their Lives* (Copenhagen: International Work Group for Indigenous Affairs, 2000), 138.

20

135 Chris Bright writes, "But the biggest obstacle to reinventing our-selves": "A History of Our Future," in *State of the World 2003: A Worldwatch Institute Report on Progress Toward a Sustainable Society* (New York: W.W. Norton, 2003), 9.

137 Subcommandante Marcos says, "History written by Power": "Flowers, Like Hope, Are Harvested," in Juana Ponce de Leon, ed., *Our Word Is Our Weapon: Selected Writings* (New York: Seven Stories Press, 2001), 173.

137 Henry David Thoreau, *Walden and Other Writings* (New York: Modern Library, 1937), 613.